Clearing the Waters

A Monograph on Saint Cyprian Divination
From the 17th to the 19th Century

Hardcover edition printed by Biddles, Norfolk.
First published in 2022.
Hadean Press Limited
Unit 30, Mantra House
South Street, Keighley
West Yorkshire
Bd21 1SX
England
www.hadeanpress.com

PUBLISHED WITH THE SUPPORT OF:

UNIÃO EUROPEIA
Fundo Social Europeu

REPÚBLICA
PORTUGUESA

CIÊNCIA, TECNOLOGIA
E ENSINO SUPERIOR

FCT
Fundação
para a Ciência
e a Tecnologia

C H S C
CENTER FOR THE
HISTORY OF SOCIETY
AND CULTURE

Clearing the Waters

A Monograph on Saint Cyprian Divination
From the 17th to the 19th Century

José Leitão

Contents

Introduction to a Historical Problem *7*

Expanding Methods, Contexts, and Databases *19*

Ritual Description *25*

From Hydromancy to Cartomancy to Text *33*

Conclusions *57*

Appendix 1A: 'System of casting cards', from the contemporary *Book of St. Cyprian* *61*

Appendix 1B: 'Way of reading the cards exactly like St. Cyprian did', from the contemporary *Book of St. Cyprian* *67*

Appendix 1C: 'Crossed Cartomancy', from the contemporary *Book of St. Cyprian* *73*

Appendix 2A: Known Saint Cyprian hydromancy references with complete incantations and ritual procedures *83*

Appendix 2B: Known Saint Cyprian hydromancy references with absent or incomplete ritual procedures *101*

Appendix 2C: Known Saint Cyprian hydromancy references with absent or fragmented incantations *103*

Appendix 2D: Known Saint Cyprian hydromancy references with incomplete or absent ritual procedures and incantations *111*

Appendix 2E: Castro Marim Saint Simeon hydromancy reference *115*

Appendix 3: Devotions of Saint Erasmus *117*

Appendix 4A: Alternative fava baptism *129*

Appendix 4B: Alternative fava casting incantation *131*

Bibliography *133*

Index *139*

INTRODUCTION TO A HISTORICAL PROBLEM

It is known that books of magic identified with the name of Saint Cyprian have existed in the Portuguese territory since at least the seventeenth century (with the first known mention being from the Inquisition trial of Pedro Afonso, from 1621).[1] From the sparse information on these early *Books*, it can be seen that their original concerns were largely those of health and the banishment of evil, just as the 'Prayer of St. Cyprian', a talismanic prayer part of a wider 'Western' magico-religious arsenal, was used as a method for the banishment of evil spirits, sorcery, and the evil eye in regions as varied as Italy,[2] Scandinavia,[3] and the Arabic world.[4] It is further known that throughout the eighteenth century, the title of 'Book of Saint Cyprian' became mostly, though not exclusively, associated with treasure hunting, where the 'Prayer of St. Cyprian' was utilized as a method for the banishment of dangerous treasure-guarding spirits. Arriving a century later at the printing press, this fluid set of written material quickly became crystallized into a mostly stable form, to which a variety of material from other sources was added: from erudite and academic Portuguese or Italian authors, French notions of nineteenth century occultism, and several collections of magical procedures of a clear and historical folk origin. Thus, the book that, today, any individual might acquire in a Portuguese bookstore as a 'Book of St. Cyprian' is

---

1 See ANTT, Inquisição de Coimbra, *Processo nr. 5634.*

2 Duni, 'Esorcisti o Stregoni?', 273.

3 Björn Gårdbäck, 'Cyprianus Förmaning', 36–50.

4 Basset, *Les Apocryphes Éthiopiens – IV*, 6–24, 38–52.

a nineteenth century production of uncertain authorship,[5] most often entitled *O Grande Livro de S. Cypriano ou Thesouro do Feiticeiro* (*The Great Book of St. Cyprian or the Sorcerer's Treasure*), containing within it a variety of different magical practices, identifiable with different backgrounds and time frames.

The writing of the history of such a book then becomes a multilayered task. There is the history of the *Book of Saint Cyprian* as a concept and idea, dealing with folk perceptions, mnemohistory, and the history of its understanding and prohibition by theologically informed institutions; the history of actual *Books of Saint Cyprian*, their origins, authors, and genealogical relations; and the history of the contents and individual elements within these books, their several sources, and how and why those elements change and evolve between books. These three levels of history, as well as all the others not enumerated, all communicate with one another and mutually influence each other. Besides these, there are further issues of religious and political history, sociologic and economic shifts, developments in technology and education, and a variety of different history-dependent disciplines which can be further brought into consideration.

A book of such sprawling historiography and fragmentary nature naturally possesses an off-beat variability of content, and it is likely this character that has garnered the contemporary *Book of Saint Cyprian* countless admirers and fans. On the other hand, this same variability is equally off-putting, as large swathes of content found in the contemporary *Book* are not responsive to, or viable in, the current age. Still, within this book, a particular set of instructions—perhaps due to their relative simplicity, straightforward applicability, and rapid results—have proven to be of universal preference and reference for contemporary

---

5 Castro Vicente, 'O Libro de San Cibrán', 95.

Cyprian-inspired practitioners, perhaps even more so since this Iberian and South American literary phenomenon was made accessible to an international readership in 2014 by Hadean Press under the title *The Book of St. Cyprian: The Sorcerer's Treasure*. The cartomancy systems within the *Book*, since its introduction to an Anglophone audience, have been among the most frequently mentioned in opinion essays, internet blog posts, professional cartomancer repertoires, and novel publications.[6] This same attractiveness is clearly not a new or specifically Anglophone phenomenon, as card divination has long been a particularly iconic aspect of the Portuguese *Book*, featuring in the cover illustrations of most of its nineteenth-century versions, such as that published by the Livraria Economica.

---

6 See Barthold, *Cyprianic Cartomancy*, for example.

The current version of the *Book of Saint Cyprian* contains three sections detailing two cartomancy systems, meaning that two of these sections describe the same system. The first of these can be found in the *Book*'s first part, originally presented as the 'System of Casting Cards' (Appendix 1A), and, later in the same section, as the 'Way of reading the cards exactly like St. Cyprian did' (Appendix 1B). The second cartomancy system is found in the *Book*'s second part, and is given the name 'Crossed Cartomancy' (Appendix 1C).

Of the two systems, 'Crossed Cartomancy' is the simplest. In very basic terms, it is performed with a deck of forty cards, from the aces to the sevens of each suit, plus the twelve court cards. Each card has a specific signification, with the pip cards mostly representing events and occurrences and the court cards representing people, which must be chosen according to the real-life people involved in the question the reading is meant to solve, there not being a necessity to include all court cards into the reading. The aces and the sevens are here referred to as the 'temptations', and these are shuffled together and placed on the table face-down. All other cards are shuffled and also placed face-down in the form of a cross with its four arms meeting the 'temptations' at the center. This spread is accompanied by a prayer, and once all the cards are cast, another prayer follows. The reading is done by flipping the cards in a particular order, working the several meanings and identities of all the cards into a narrative, what Jake Stratton-Kent has referred to as 'text generation'.[7] The reading is done in steps of nine cards, and should the question under divination be answered by any group of nine, no further cards need to be read.

---

7 Stratton-Kent, 'Seven Years the Sea Thou Roamed', 166.

The other cartomancy system of the *Book* once again uses a forty-card deck, the same as that of 'Crossed Cartomancy'. The cards are given different significations, but overall the same distinction between pip and court cards still applies, there simply being the difference that all the court cards should be used and some of these might not refer to people, but rather to their thoughts. In order to work this system, one first needs to shuffle and break the cards into five piles, displaying them as a cross and praying a Response over them. After this, the cards are collected and cast into five columns of eight cards each. In this disposition the reader is meant to go through every card in a particular order, once again generating a narrative of people and events.

A particular complication might arise in this system should one find that the middle column does not contain any court cards. This is referred to as a 'novelty', and must be solved with a different spread. In that case, all the cards except the eight in this middle column are collected and a particular incantation is said:

> Cards, by the power of St. Cyprian, who seven years the sea roamed, and seven [lots] for his divine wife he cast, tell me if this man is keeping himself faithful and loyal to this woman.[8]

Out of the newly collected cards, twenty-one are spread over the column of eight, eight are placed in the form of a cross to the side of these, and three remain in the reader's hand. One then proceeds to, once again, read the cards with

---

8 'Cartas, pelo poder de S. Cypriano, que sete annos no mar andou, e sete sortes por sua divina esposa deitou, dizei-me se este senhor guarda fé e lealdade a esta senhora', in Anon., *O Grande Livro de S. Cypriano*, part 1, 77; Leitão, *The Book of St. Cyprian*, 51.

exactly the same significations as given before, starting with the three in one's hand, moving on to the eight on the side, and ending with the remaining twenty-one. It is further suggested that, should at any point the question being divined be resolved by any one of these three groups, one does not then need to move on to the next group. Further complication may be added in either of these systems by the individual practitioner, particularly regarding the standard prescribed meaning of each card, but, as far as the *Book* presents them, these are simple and no-nonsense methods of acquiring unambiguous information about a particular problem.

While all of this is an argument for the clarity of these forms of 'Cyprianic cartomancy', some of their technical aspects are somewhat more confusing from a historical and even religious point of view. Particular among these is the incantation meant to be said in preparation for resolving the 'novelty' procedure given above. What is immediately striking about this incantation is its complete dissociation from cartomancy or playing cards in general within its own narrative and thematic elements. Regarding this, the second time the first cartomancy system is presented in the *Book*, the text adds a small pseudo-hagiographical narrative with the apparent purpose of offering some sort of context and justification for this very incantation. It mentions a supposed seven-year journey made by Saint Cyprian himself, where, finding himself homesick, he developed this system of cartomancy to have news of his wife, children, and loved ones. Following this, a consecration method is offered which rests on this same narrative and uses some of the same symbols mentioned in the 'novelty' incantation:

Cyprian took the deck of cards and passed them, one by one, in seven basins of holy water, each one from its own church; after this he said the Creed over them in a cross, that is, made the sign of the cross over them with his right hand. Next, he passed them through the waves of the sea, wrapped seven times so as not to get them wet.[9]

While this would be a satisfactory explanation for the 'novelty' prayer if we restricted our understanding of Saint Cyprian literature and related practices to this single book, things become more complicated when this is inserted into the general context of nineteenth-century *Books of Saint Cyprian*. An example of this comes from the ethnographer and ethnomusicologist Pedro Fernandes Tomás (1853-1927) who, while discussing folk 'superstitions' from the Figueira da Foz, offers a thematically similar incantation, equally associated with cartomancy, and likely taken from a currently unknown printed nineteenth-century *Book of Saint Cyprian*:

Blessed St. Cyprian, bishop and archbishop, my lord Jesus Christ – seven years in the sea thou roamed, seven orphans thou succored, seven times thy [lots] thou cast and asked if thy beloved was faithful; just as thou wished to know if she was faithful, so do I ask

---

9 'Cypriano pegou no baralho das cartas e foi passal-as por sete pias de agua benta, cada uma na sua egreja, depois d'isso disse sobre ellas o crédo em cruz, isto é, fez nas cartas cruzes com a mão direita, em seguida passou-as pelas ondas do mar, sete vezes embrulhadas, e não se molharam', in in Anon., *O Grande Livro de S. Cypriano*, part 1, 92; Leitão, *The Book of St. Cyprian*, 63.

thee to declare to me the lots asked in truth, by means of this deck of cards.[10]

The same once again happens with the nineteenth-century Portuguese writer Camilo Castelo Branco (1825-1890), who presents a very similar incantation in his novel *A Filha do Arcediago* (1854), once again associated with cartomancy and once again likely taken from a currently unknown printed *Book of Saint Cyprian*:

St. Cyprian, bishop and archbishop thou were, seven years in the sea thou roamed, in thy divine grace thou sustained thyself, seven lots for thy divine wife thou cast, in the end thou declared thyself. Declare to me here if Rosinha is enamored with José, son of the haberdasher.[11]

While the fragmentary nature of both accounts makes any definitive assessment difficult, it would seem that, while a seafaring Cyprian incantation is present in both instances, there is no mention of any justifying pseudo-hagiographical narrative such as the contemporary *Books* possess. Furthermore, what is

---

10 'S. Cypriano bemdito, bispo e arcebispo, meu senhor Jesus Christo – sete annos no mar andastes, sete órfãos amparastes, sete vezes a sorte deitaste e perguntaste se a vossa amada vos era leal; assim como desejaste saber se ella vos era leal, assim vos peço me declareis a sorte pedida em verdade, por meio d'este baralho de cartas', in Thomás, 'Superstições Populares do Concelho da Figueira', 27; Leitão, 'Searching for Cyprian', 132.

11 'S. Cypriano, bispo e arcebispo fostes, sete annos no mar andastes, na vossa divina graça vos sustentastes, sete sortes pela vossa divina esposa botastes, no fim vos declarastes. Declarai-me aqui se a Rosinha anda de namoro com o José filho do retroseiro', in Castello Branco, *A Filha do Arcediago*, 17.

also implied in these instances is that this incantation is meant to be used as a preliminary step to the cartomancy reading itself, and not to a rather small technicism within the procedure.

Complicating the case further is the presence of these same types of incantations in purely folk environments, as identified by the ethnographer José Leite de Vasconcelos (1858-1941), placing any strict relation between the above pseudo-hagiographical consecration narrative and these recurrent incantations in serious doubt. In these folk environments, this consecration is never presented as a mandatory step in the performance of the divinatory procedures the incantations in question are otherwise associated with, and no pseudo-hagiographical justification for the incantation is ever given besides the prayer itself. Furthermore, Vasconcelos doesn't attribute these incantations to any specific form of divination, potentially meaning that these were not associated with cartomancy in the environments where he observed them:

St. Cyprian,
Seven years the sea thou roamed,
To learn news of thy lady
Seven [lots] thou threw in…
Thy luck thou took out right…
I ask thee now my dearest miraculous saint,
That thou discover this for me.[12]

My St. Cyprian
My dearest St. Cyprian,
My sorcerer

---

12 'S. Cipriano, / Sete anos no mar andastes, / Para saberes notícias da vossa dama / Sete sortes botastes… / A vossa sorte saíu certa… / Peço-vos, milagroso santinho / Que me faças esta descoberta', in Vasconcelos, *Opúsculos*, vol. 5, 592; Leitão, *The Book of St. Cyprian*, 301.

My dearest sorcerer,
In the sea thou roamed,
Eleven virgins did thou find,
With them did thou speak,
Thou ate and thou drank;
Thy [lots] thou threw in,
Better did thou take it out:
Tell me now mine
To know if I am to be married[13]

Consequently, the origin and meaning of these thematically coherent incantations, as related to Cyprian cartomancy systems (or any other 'Cyprianic' divination method), remains unresolved. These are incantations which are found associated with cartomancy, but this association is not clear, neither in terms of attributes nor symbolism, and even if the contemporary *Book of Saint Cyprian* offers a narrative justification for this association, it remains the single known source that does so. While one might consider this satisfactory within a limited scope, this same narrative, with its explicit binding of these incantations to cartomancy, actually sets itself up to be radically contradicted when the same incantations are found potentially associated with other forms of non-cartomancy divination, irrefutably identifying the narrative as a false historical origin. But still, the recurrence and thematic coherence of these five instances is a sign of deliberateness and meaning, and, as expertly put by Rustin Cohle, meaning is historical. One is then left with

---

13 'Meu S. Supriano / Meu S. Suprianinho, / Meu feiticeiro, / Meu feiticeirinho, / No mar andastes, / Onze virges encontrastes, / Com ellas fallastes, / Comestes, e bubestes; / Vossa sorte botastes, / Milhor a tirastes: / Dizei-me agora a minha / P'ra saber se casarei', in Vasconcelos, *Tradições Populares de Portugal*, 305; Leitão, *The Book of St. Cyprian*, 301.

the following straightforward questions: what is this seafaring incantation, what do its symbols mean, and how does it find itself contemporarily associated with cartomancy. Thus, this is one of the several items within the contemporary *Book* for which a history can be written.

EXPANDING METHODS, CONTEXTS, AND DATABASES

The folk origin of this divination incantation is a clue to the discovery of its ultimate source and meaning. Such should not be a surprise as, through careful examination of the nineteenth-century works of Vasconcelos and other ethnographers, much of the general content of the contemporary *Book* can be identified as having a folk origin, seeing as several items within the text are equally found in purely oral rural practices. However, the clear delimitation of this same 'folk', be it in geographical, chronological, or cultural terms, was (and is) always a problem. Often the attribution of the label 'folk' to any cultural item represents an implicit disregard for its origins, and it can also be used as an umbrella term which shields one from the responsibility of further research. Like the Eliadian 'archaic', if something is labeled 'folk' then it no longer needs to be detailed or scrutinized, as it becomes the possession of the ancestral 'rustics' and beyond academic or historical inquiry. This can perhaps explain the appalling state of Portuguese academic esoteric or magical studies, as the shadow of men such as Vasconcelos has given many the justification to excuse themselves from any further research which might endanger the works of their masters.

Yet, continuing research into the history of the *Book* has revealed that 'the folk' are not an opaque, unreachable, and inscrutable intellectual group. Many of the text's loose ends, the various items in its lists of apparently unrelated magical practices, sorceries, incantations, and talismans can be consistently found in several Portuguese Inquisition documents relating to a particular style of early modern magical practice which might be referred to as 'urban folk magic'. Thus, folk culture, from which the *Book* extracts large portions of its content, is, obviously, historical and contextual, not 'archaic', and can be studied as such. In fact, this magical culture has, in a way, already been studied by the Inquisitors who persecuted its practices in the past and left a record of their research.

From the data collected in the archives of the Portuguese Inquisition, urban folk magic essentially comprised an oral tradition found throughout urban centers in Portugal, Spain, and Brazil,[14] echoes of which can still be heard in the many Luso-Afro-American cults of Brazil, such as Umbanda and Quimbanda. From the research so far conducted, between the dates of 1619 and 1758, a total of eighty-seven urban folk magic Inquisition trials can be found, solely located in the city of Lisbon. These cases are typically characterized by a great focus on erotic/dominating and harmful sorcery, various forms of divination to determine a lover's/spouse's thoughts and whereabouts, and recourse to a somewhat coherent and recurrent roster of (Christian) saints and demons. Iconic among these are the names of the trinity of Barrabás, Caifás, and Satanás (several variations possible), Maria de Padilha (a spirit whose name is first found in trials related to Castilian immigrants but who gradually travels to the 'mainstream'), Saint Erasmus, Saint Leonard, Saint Anne, Saint Helen, Marta the wicked/lost and, to a much lesser degree, Saint Cyprian.

Socially speaking, the practitioners of this form of magic tended to organize themselves in loose and fragmentary groups which would occasionally gather in order to trade new magical procedures, rare *materia magica*, and clients, there being a great fluidity between the categories of 'client' and 'colleague'. These

---

14 See Bethencourt, *O Imaginário da Magia*; Paiva, *Bruxaria e Superstição*; Tausiet, *Urban Magic in Early Modern Spain*; Souza, *The Devil and the Land of the Holy Cross*.

gatherings should not be confused with Romantic ideas of the witches' sabbat or other such demonological constructions; these were essentially professional gatherings where business and working methodologies were traded and discussed. In terms of gender, such a style of magic was overwhelmingly performed by women, with eighty-one of the above-mentioned eighty-seven cases pertaining to defendants of that gender. In particular, it should be noted that these same magic practitioners tended to belong to vulnerable and marginal social groups, namely, widows, prostitutes, sailors' wives, immigrants, and the illicit lovers of noblemen, collectively referred to as 'mulheres erradas', wrong/evil women, or 'mulheres de trato/vida ruim', women of bad dealing/life, and that such loose organizations of practitioners essentially functioned as social networks of solidarity and mutual aid.

Cosmologically speaking, the 'inner logic', or the methods and techniques utilized in this style of magic, can be interpreted as religiously subversive, meaning they relied upon non-normalized methods for the manipulation of cosmological aspects of the local dominant religion. Thus, these practices cannot be considered anti-religious or 'anti-cosmic', much less as evidence of an alternative religion in open competition with Christianity/Catholicism. On the contrary, these practices were entirely dependent on the cosmic reality of Catholicism for their ontological foundation. They depended entirely on the existence of a Heaven, Hell, and Purgatory populated with saints, evil spirits, and needy souls according to a Catholic conception, as well as on the effectiveness of the sacraments and Catholic *materia sacra*. Thus, these practices are better understood as a form of socially contextualized early modern Catholicism.

While the concept of 'The Book of St. Cyprian' is, historically, one emerging from the rural Portuguese North, and the contemporary *Book* is, undoubtedly, an object of the nineteenth century, the *Book* itself is also a historically legitimate expression of this same style of early modern magic and religiosity, and many of its magical procedures can often be found, word-for-word, in the same Lisbon Inquisition documents detailing practitioners of urban folk magic. Yet, the continuity between the contemporary *Book* and the practices described in these trials is shadowed by the rare mention of Saint Cyprian within them. While the figure of Saint Cyprian is placed, at least as early as the seventeenth century, as the patron of the most important local Iberian grimoire tradition, his name is rarely found among the magical practices from which the *Book*'s current content emerges. Apart from mentions or variations of the 'Prayer of St. Cyprian', from the documentation so far studied, Cyprian's name is only featured or implied in eight Inquisition trials. Noticeably, all of these mentions are associated with divination, and in particular, all except one focuses on hydromancy.

It is here the significance of the cartomancy incantations discussed above begins to become clear. Out of these eight trials, five also feature an incantation with the same theme and elements as the one present in the contemporary *Book* for the resolution of the 'novelty' event. Not only this, but in the seven hydromancy rituals present here, the several elements mentioned in these incantations, which in the cartomancy system appear disjointed from its other symbols or ritual enactment, all refer to specific acts and objects necessary for this same kind of hydromancy ritual. The waves of the sea refer to the water upon which the seer gazes; the lots cast into the water refer to straws which should be cast into the vessel before divination can commence; and the lady/virgin(s), although uncertain, likely refer to the virgin seer necessary to perform the divination.

Arriving at this point, the origin and understanding of the cartomancy incantations from the contemporary *Book* should now become clear. The current incarnation of the Portuguese *Book of Saint Cyprian* traces significant portions of its content to early modern Portuguese urban folk magic; in this style of magic, even if rare, the name of Saint Cyprian is most often found associated with hydromancy and a somewhat coherent and recurrent verbal incantation. As hydromancy fell out of use in favor of cartomancy, the appeal to Cyprian simply shifted from one form of divination to the other and, likely out of habit, its associated incantation was maintained.

Yet, even if logical, this explanation leaves many further problems to be resolved. First of all, the small sample size of seven trial records does not allow for a deep understanding of all the possible variations or nuances of this hydromancy ritual. More importantly, it does not explain how the name of Cyprian migrated from hydromancy to cartomancy, or the several other particularities of the current cartomancy system, such as the historical meaning of its 'text generation'.

These problems can begin to be resolved by a broadening of the databases investigated. It should be pointed out that the several hundreds of trials pertaining to magical practice (be it urban, rural, folk, or learned) collected by the Portuguese Inquisition are in fact a somewhat minor aspect of the entirety of the documentation produced by that institution. Parallel to the trial records, one also finds what are called the *Cadernos do Promotor*, or the *Prosecutor's Notebooks*: large, massive books where any and all documents, denunciations, confessions, and investigations which did not give rise to a formal trial were stored.

Counterbalancing the trials, the investigation so far conducted into these extensive tomes reveals a much greater number of mentions (be they direct or implied) of the name of 'Saint Cyprian' as associated with urban folk magic; in total, a further eighteen instances, all of which related to hydromancy. Further research into the Portuguese National Library has also found one other instance of this same ritual, inconspicuously copied in the back of an early seventeenth-century book by the Jesuit João Delgado (1553-1612), astrology master at the college of Santo Antão in Lisbon. Further complicating things, one more ritual, hailing from the southern Portuguese town of Castro Marim, has also been found which, while being entirely coherent with the Saint Cyprian rituals, calls upon Saint Simeon instead. Castro Marim, it should be noted, was a location to which the Inquisitorial condemned were frequently exiled, meaning that the occurrence of this strange variation in this remote location could have a countless number of origins. Adding these numbers up elevates the number of new Cyprian hydromancy rituals to nineteen, the total of known Cyprian hydromancy rituals to twenty-six, and the total number of 'lots in the sea thou cast' rituals to twenty-seven.

Ritual Description

Focusing on the twenty-six Saint Cyprian procedures, fourteen of them might be considered to be complete, meaning they apparently contain full ritual instructions and a complete incantation to accompany them (Appendix 2A); one features solely an incantation (Appendix 2B); seven appear to only contain full ritual proceedings, being accompanied by either apparently fragmented incantations, or none at all (Appendix 2C); and the remaining four seem to be made up of both fragmented ritual proceedings and fragmented incantations (Appendix 2D). The Saint Simeon procedures appears to contain a complete ritual and incantation (Appendix 2E).

While it addresses a different saint, the Saint Simeon ritual is clearly a part of the same general continuum of urban folk magic hydromancy as the Saint Cyprian rituals. The phonetic similarity between Simeon and Cyprian (particularly in their possible Portuguese variations, such as 'Semeam' and 'Cepriam', or even 'Cebriam') could easily be taken to indicate that 'Simeon' here is but a corruption of the proper 'Cyprian'. Yet, the attribution of the label of 'corruption' to this single instance, while being based on a solid statistical observation, is still a gross imprecision. As procedures arising from a particular expression of folk oral culture, none of these can be considered as 'purer' or more 'corrupt' than any others, as folk oral culture exists in a constant state of fluidity and variation. Practices of this sort only become fixed in a particular orthodoxy, or 'correct form', when these are placed down in written form.

To now try to break down the several elements within this ritual, all twenty-seven instances will be taken into consideration.

This is not to mean that we are simply assuming that the Simeon ritual is merely an offshoot of the Cyprian one, but rather that these are all different legitimate steps in the history and variability of this ritual.

As mentioned, the ritual, particularly its incantation, is largely consistent throughout all known instances, although there is a suggestion of increasing complexity over time. At the base of this ritual stands a chamber pot. Other water containers are also possible, but this is stressed in one instance as being the best and most appropriate for the operation in question.[15]

Alongside the chamber pot, one should have several straws, which should have been cut and prepared beforehand. The origin of these straws does not seem to be important, as they are alternately described as being taken from a mat or cut from reeds. These straws represent the 'lots' mentioned in the incantation. There is one mention of this being solely one straw,[16] two mentions of these same straws being two in number,[17] and two instances of them being seven,[18] the number found in the contemporary versions of this incantation presented above. However, the most common number, with at least nineteen mentions, is nine, with one further instance being uncertain whether the number is nine or three.[19] Nine is also one of the numbers most commonly associated with Saint Cyprian in contemporary international magical practices,[20] and in one instance the number nine is also mentioned as representing

---

15 ANTT, Inquisição de Lisboa, *57° Caderno do Promotor*, fol.591v.

16 ANTT, Inquisição de Évora, *38° Caderno do Promotor*, fol.192r.

17 ANTT, Inquisição de Lisboa, *3° Caderno do Promotor*, fol.362v; ANTT, *36° Caderno do Promotor*, fol.4v.

18 ANTT, Inquisição de Lisboa, *37° Caderno do Promotor*, fol.532r.

19 ANTT, Inquisição de Lisboa, *47° Caderno do Promotor*, fol.310v.

20 Ali, *Saint Cyprian*, 4.

the number of days Saint Cyprian was lost at sea,[21] indicating the presence of pseudo-hagiographical narratives circulating among practitioners.

Once filled with water, the chamber pot might be placed over a plate with salt, likely to represent the salt of the sea. This step is only mentioned in five instances from the late seventeenth and eighteenth century, all of which are relatively late practices when compared with the majority of the known rituals. One other rare variation is the placing of the pot under the light of the sun, mentioned three times.

The straws are taken and dropped one at a time inside the pot, and for each straw one should pray the incantation. Two documents offer a potential variation on this point, in that the straws should be cast two at a time, bent like crosses[22] (possibly indicating the use of more than nine straws in order to make the crosses), and two other instances also mention that, instead of casting any straws, they should simply be placed over the pot in the form of a cross.[23] Another step, present in seven instances and which is likely related to this last preoccupation, is the placement of an open pair of scissors over the mouth of the pot in the form of a cross, this being sometimes accompanied by covering the mouth of the pot with a napkin or tissue, present in four instances. Finally, in two instances an egg is also used, in one case being cast into the pot together with nine straws,[24] and

21 ANTT, Inquisição de Lisboa, *Processo nr. 7020*, fol.20v.

22 ANTT, Inquisição de Lisboa, *Processo nr. 8877*, fol.16r; ANTT, Inquisição de Lisboa, *Processo nr. 7020*, fol.20r.

23 ANTT, Inquisição de Lisboa, *3º Caderno do Promotor*, fol.363r; ANTT, Inquisição de Évora, *38º Caderno do Promotor*, fol.192r.

24 ANTT, Inquisição de Lisboa, *Processo nr. 1082*, fol.40v.

in the other as their replacement, even though the incantation used in that instance still mentions nine lots.[25]

Before the incantation is uttered, one instance suggests that five Our Fathers and five Hail Marys should be prayed over the water, using a rosary.[26] The incantation itself does not stray excessively from the contemporary versions, and all its known early modern variations may be consulted in Appendix 2. However, a number of significant differences are noticeable and a few of these carry with them important implications for the understanding and functioning of the procedure. The first peculiarity of the early modern incantations is the opening line of eleven of them, calling on Saint Cyprian/Simeon as 'bishop and archbishop', an expression also sometimes followed by 'confessor of (the house) of my lord Jesus Christ' or just 'Jesus Christ'. This, out of all known contemporary iterations, is only present in the Camilo Castelo Branco version.

On a superficial note, this opening seems to, first and foremost, provide some of the rhythm and rhyme scheme of the incantations, making the Portuguese 'Bispo/Arcebispo' rhyme with 'Cristo'. This same opening can also be found associated with other saints within the urban folk magic *milieu*, most noticeably with Saint Erasmus. Overall, as stated above, Saint Erasmus is an extremely popular saint in Portuguese urban folk magic, and is typically petitioned for the domination of a potential lover through what is known as the Prayer or Devotion of Saint Erasmus (Appendix 3). This is an extremely lengthy prayer, usually performed while gazing at an image of the martyrdom of Erasmus, and it intends to transmit the same tortures and suffering of martyrdom depicted in the image onto its target. Alternatively, one single instance is also known of a

---

25 ANTT, Inquisição de Lisboa, *Processo nr. 7485*, fol.76r.

26 ANTT, Inquisição de Évora, *38º Caderno do Promotor*, fol.192r.

chamber pot hydromancy ritual which appeals to Erasmus.[27] Although no other technicalities or incantation details regarding this particular rite are given, such a practice probably relies on a certain passage of his 'regular' devotion which mentions the casting of Erasmus's intestines into the sea. Still, the presence of this opening in the Cyprian hydromancy incantations could be an indication of mutual influence between both these practices (something which should be considered common in what was essentially an oral magical tradition), or simply a common and efficient way to address any male saint in the context of Portuguese urban folk magic.

One other aspect that is continuously stressed in the early modern incantation, as well as in the description of the full rituals given by many of the testimonies and confessions, is the necessary presence of a virgin, or the evocation of one's own virginity. This is an aspect of the practice which is not particularly stressed in the contemporary versions of the ritual, as it is likely the most technically difficult aspect to be recreated in an increasingly complex society. Overall, the necessity of the virginity of the seer is described in a total of fifteen instances, be it in the description of the ritual procedures and those performing them, or the very incantation—this against twelve instances where no such necessity is mentioned. The fulfillment of this requirement frequently means the presence of a young child, typically a girl, who should have either previously memorized the incantation, or be coached on-site for her role. Still, this aspect of the procedure is offered a certain leeway in a limited number of denunciations. In one of these, from 1625, while 'virginity' was something still invoked in the incantation, the virgin in question did not need to be the seer, but rather just someone present at the time of the performance, a modification

---

27 ANTT, Inquisição de Lisboa, *75° Caderno do Promotor*, fol.5r.

which could be accomplished by some mild tampering with the typical wording of the incantation from 'by thy sanctity and my virginity' to 'by thy sanctity and by the virginity of this girl'.[28] Alternatively, the incantation and ritual procedure itself could be further changed in order to evoke an alternative to 'virginity'. In a 1704 denunciation of this ritual being performed by two women of whom only one was a virgin, the incantation offered evokes both the virginity and chastity of the seer(s) by using the wording: 'by thy sanctity, with my chastity, with my virginity'.[29] In this instance, when the word 'chastity' was uttered, the non-virgin seer would place her hand over the chamber pot, the same being done by the virgin seer upon the pronunciation of the word 'virginity',[30] suggesting that a non-virgin could indeed perform this ritual or at least actively participate in it.

This is further confirmed by an earlier denunciation from 1684, where it is explicitly mentioned that the wording of the incantation should be chosen in accordance with the virgin or non-virgin status of the seer, being that 'virginity' should be substituted by 'chastity' when the seer was not a 'damsel'.[31] Yet another alternative is given by a single instance from 1624, where the standard incantation was broken by the seer in order for her to perform an impromptu confession over the chamber pot,[32] suggesting that this was done so that the seer would acquire some form of perceived 'purity' somewhat akin to virginity/chastity and be able to perform the divination.

28 'pella vossa sanctidade e pella vergindade desta menina', in ANTT, Inquisição de Lisboa, *7º Caderno do Promotor*, fol.346v.

29 'p^la vossa santidade com minha casthidade, com minha virgindade vos pesso', in ANTT, Inquisição de Lisboa, *80º Caderno do Promotor*, fol.262v.

30 ANTT, Inquisição de Lisboa, *80º Caderno do Promotor*, fol.263r.

31 ANTT, Inquisição de Lisboa, *81º Caderno do Promotor*, fol.322r.

32 ANTT, Inquisição de Lisboa, *7º Caderno do Promotor*, fol.516r.

After the standard incantation is performed, further prayers are prescribed in seven instances. These are once again standard Christian/Catholic prayers, such as the Our Father, Hail Mary, and the Creed, occasionally accompanied by the making of crosses over the mouth of the chamber pot. Particular details about these prayers are offered in one instance, where it is mentioned that such prayers were meant to be offered to Saint Cyprian and, furthermore, besides these, after the entire procedure, the chamber pot should be exorcized of any potential negative influence with the words 'if thou has an active or passive pact, of all I renounce'.[33] The one instance where prayers are offered before the incantation likely addresses these same preoccupations.

As mentioned above, the incantation and its accompanying prayers should be said for each one of the straws cast into the pot, after which the seer would gaze into the water in order to have a vision. However, two instances do deviate from this point by suggesting that the answers given by this method of divination were not strictly visionary, but also analogical. In one of these, besides seeking a vision of a seaman in the waters, it is mentioned that the state of health and location of this same man could be discovered if the straws came to the edges of the chamber pot, this being 'a sign that her mentioned husband was on land',[34] and in one of the procedures where only an egg is used (instead of straws) the answer was rather sought in the shapes the free-flowing yolk and egg white would make inside the pot.[35]

---

33 'se tu tens pacto activo, ou passivo, de todo o renuncio', in ANTT, Inquisição de Lisboa, *Processo nr. 9809*, fol.5v.

34 'era sinal que o ditto seu marido estava em terra', in ANTT, Inquisição de Lisboa, *Processo nr. 7020*, fol.43v.

35 ANTT, Inquisição de Lisboa, *Processo nr. 7485*, fol.76v.

Noticeably, the majority of questions addressed in this form of divination tended to deal with the determination of the health status, survival, or fidelity of traveling or seafaring men. In this way, it filled a very specific purpose within the extensive arsenal of the early modern Portuguese urban folk magician, which could help explain why this was never the most common divination used within this magical *milieu*. Overall, general questions on love, wealth, or any other mundane preoccupation could be much more easily addressed by any other form of divination, and this one, given its clear seafaring motif, was likely relegated to questions concerning seafaring travelers.

FROM HYDROMANCY TO CARTOMANCY TO TEXT

Once again returning to the general analysis of the presence of Saint Cyprian in early modern urban folk magic, besides these hydromancy rituals, there are a limited number of such instances and they are still associated with divination. Once again, this is excluding instances of the use of the 'Prayer of Saint Cyprian'.

Variations on this prayer are also known, as it can be further used in the composition of *Bolsas de Mandinga*, complex magical talismans of a truly Atlantic nature, bearing elements from magical practices of Africa, America, and Europe, or, in truncated forms, used as a *Carta de Tocar*,[36] a kind of written talisman. It should be noted that, contrary to the regular use of the 'Prayer of Saint Cyprian' as a method of spiritual protection, both these types of talismans (*Bolsas* and *Cartas*) are explicitly meant for physical and bodily protection, with the *Bolsas* being of particular predilection among soldiers across the Portuguese Empire.

Focusing on other forms of Cyprian divination, their eighteenth-century expressions are still somewhat understudied, and it is here that, in all likelihood, the more relevant clues regarding the transition of this incantation from hydromancy to cartomancy will be found. Still, beyond the specific seafaring Cyprian divination ritual, a few more techniques can be traced. The first of these is still closely associated with this same hydromancy ritual, being distinguished only by an alternative incantation which largely breaks with the thematic and

---

36 ANTT, Inquisição de Lisboa, *Processo nr. 1550*, fol.5v

procedural coherence of the more common ritual. Interestingly, this alternative incantation is simply presented in its trial record as a potential substitute for the seafaring-themed one, and all the other ritual procedures so far presented are meant to be observed while performing it:

1743 truncated version of the Prayer of Saint Cyprian used as a Carta de Tocar. Tribunal do Santo Ofício, Inquisição de Lisboa, proc. 1550. PT/TT/TSO-IL/028/01550. "Imagem cedida pelo ANTT"

Blessed St. Cyprian who to the world thou rose, and
of herbs thou covered thyself, three shouts thou gave
for the Holiest Trinity to aid thee; and by the divine
sustenance, and by the divine sacrament I ask thee to
discover if António Rodriguez is dead or alive : which
once all was done, the felon placed a scissor as a cross
on the mouth of the said chamber pot, uttering some
more words in a low voice, which she said were of the
Creed (...)[37]

Completely breaking away from hydromancy is a rather
unique 1673 procedure explicitly mentioned as 'being good to
learn all one may wish to know, both hidden and future things',
as given by Paula de Moura:[38]

(...) both of them on their knees, in front of an altar,
which was done over a table covered with towels, and
on it three saints outlined, Saint Elias, Saint Mark,
and Saint Cyprian, without any lit candles or lamps,
[she did] the following devotion; that she should pray
fifteen Our Fathers, and fifteen Hail Marys, and that
the said devotion was good for the said effect, and that
before she started praying the said prayers she should

---

37 'Bem aventurado S. Cypriano q̃ ao mundo subistes, e de ervas
vos cobristes, tres bràdos destes pla Sma Trinde, q̃ vos acodisse; e plo
divino sustento, e plo divino sacramto vos pesso q̃ me descobrais se
he morto, ou vivo Anto Rioz : o q̃ tudo feito pòz a delata hũa tezoura
em cruz na boca do dto ourinol, proferindo mais outras palavras em
voz baixa, q̃ disse serem do Credo', in ANTT, Inquisição de Lisboa,
Processo nr. 1082, fol.41r; Leitão, *Opuscula Cypriani*, 96.

38 'era boa para se saber tudo quando se quizesse saber, assim de
couzas occultas, como futuras', in ANTT, Inquisição de Lisboa,
Processo nr. 5723, fol.34v.

take a small clay bowl, and casting into this vinegar, and some grains of pepper, and place this over a lit stove near her in honor of the martyrdoms that the mentioned saints suffered, and cast inside this a small piece of white/blank paper, and if what they wanted to happen was to happen, the said paper would come to the top of the boiling, and that she further cast into the said bowl three needles in honor of the Holiest Trinity, and that the said devotion should be started when there rang the eight hours in the morning, and finish at nine, and that the said hour should be spent with her the confessant on her knees in front of the said saints, and altar, and near her the said stove with the said things, and praying the said fifteen Our Fathers, and fifteen Hail Marys, with her hands raised towards the mentioned saints (…)[39]

---

39 'pondosse ambas de joelhos, deante de hum altar, que estava feito sobre huma meza cuberta com toalhas, e nelle tres santos de vulto, a saber, Santo Elias, Saõ Marcos, e Saõ Cipriano, sem ter velas, ou candea acezas, a devoçaõ seguinte; que rezasse aos ditos santos quinze Padres nossos, e quinze Ave Marias, e que a ditta devoçaõ era boa para o ditto effeito, e que antes de começar a rezar as dittas oraçoẽs havia de tomar huma tijella pequena de barro, e lançando-lhe vinagre, e huns graõs de pimenta a pozesse em hum fugareiro acezo junto de sy á honra dos martyrios que os ditos santos padeceraõ, e lhe lançasse dentro hum pequeno de papel branco, e se houvesse de suceder o que se prettendia, havia o ditto papel vir a sima do ditto cozimento, e que lhe lançasse mais na ditta tigela tres alfinetes á honra da Santissima Trindade, e que a ditta devoção se havia de fazer dandolhe principio tanto que dessem oito horas da manhã, e acabar ás nove, e que a ditta hora se havia de passar estando ella confitente de joelhos diante dos ditos santos, e altar, e junto della o ditto fugareiro com as dittas couzas, e rezendo os dittos quinze Padre nossos, e quinze Ave Marias com as maõs levantadas para os ditos santos', in ANTT, Inquisição de Lisboa, *Processo nr. 5723*, fol.34v-35r.

This procedure is further mentioned by Paula de Moura in a later and unrelated confession present in a *Caderno*. In this second account, this trinity of Saints is instead mentioned as being 'Saint Friar Isidore', 'Saint Friar Cyprian', and Saint Mark.[40] While the reference to Saint Isidore is, at this point, without particular interest, the other two extra saints addressed in this devotion should be highlighted. Saint Mark is another popular saint in Iberian and South American magical practices, largely associated with the capture and domination of wills and hearts (a position also occupied by Saint Cyprian, Saint Gonçalo, Saint John, and the Corpus Christi).[41] Saint Elias might be a reference to the prophet Elijah, but what is implied is probably something more ambiguous. This same name can equally be found in an incantation associated with another divination procedure of 'seeking voices', the search for answers to a question based on random words heard on the street or during specific religious ceremonies, collected by Vasconcelos in Lisbon:[42]

F. . . ., where are thou and where am I? Neither does thou see me, nor do I see thee; I have for thee what thou does not have for me; three messengers, all of them strong – Lucas, Luzes and Elias. There I send them to thee, so as they may do in thy heart such a revolution and such a love for me that thou will not be able to eat, nor drink, nor sleep, nor rest, if thou does not speak to me. Lucas, Luzes and Elias, if this is such, signs thou should give me: dogs barking, doors opening

---

40 ANTT, Inquisição de Lisboa, *50° Caderno do Promotor*, fol.429r.

41 Azzi, 'O Casamento na Sociedade Colonial Luso-Brasileira', 51; See Leitão, *The Book of St. Cyprian*, 373-376.

42 See Leitão, 'Seeking Voices and Finding Meaning'.

and closing, bells ringing and boys crying, while I pray
nine Salve Reginas in thy name.[43]

In this case, while the presence of the name Elias might be,
firstly, taken to be associated with the alliteration it establishes
with Lucas (Luke) and Luzes (Lights), this last name is likely
a corruption, contraction, or fill-in for Lucifer, suggesting that
these are the names of evil spirits. This same consideration
might be carried over to the Elias-Mark-Cyprian divination
given above.

The remaining part of this devotion—the preparation of
a mix of vinegar, pepper, and pins—is usually referred to in
urban folk magic trials as a 'boiling', an aggressive, irritating,
and foul-smelling mix of ingredients meant to spur the action
of evil spirits, most often the trinity of Satanás, Barrabás, and
Caifás, or any of its many variations, in order to torture and
torment a particular victim. There being a clear association
of Saint Mark with this same realm of action, and a minor
one with Cyprian, what is strongly suggested by this form of
divination is that these three saints are being addressed in this
particular instance as evil spirits.

Another rather late instance of Cyprianic divination is a
coscinomancy ritual found in a document from 1800, when the
Inquisition was already in its death throes. This method by itself

---

43 'F. . . ., onde estás tu e onde estou eu? Nem tu me vês a mim,
nem eu te vejo a ti; eu tenho para ti o que tu não tens para mim;
três mensageiros, todos eles muito fortes – Lucas, Luzes e Elias. Lá
tos mando, lá tos envio, para que façam no teu coração tamanha
revolução e tamanho amor por mim que não possas comer nem beber,
nem dormir, nem descansar, sem comigo vires falar. Lucas, Luzes e
Elias, se assim for, sinais me haveis de dar: cães a ladrar, portas a abrir
e a fechar, sinos a tocar e meninos a chorar, enquanto eu rezo nove
salve-rainhas por vossa intenção', in Vasconcelos, *Etnografia Portuguesa*,
vol. 9, 40.

is rather common in the context of urban folk magic, being frequently associated, as in the rest of Europe, with Saint Paul and Saint Peter, though there are rare instances where this same rite is performed by the invocation of the trinity of Barrabás, Satanás, and Caifás, and even Maria de Padilha:[44]

> (...) picking the rim of a sieve, placing a scissor, and a ten *reis* coin, and she made it spin and she said these words: By virtue of Saint Odo, Saint Cyprian, and dearest Saint Cyprian, and the eyes of owls, and a thousand trees, so as this would tell if it was certain what she was saying, if a certain Maria Joana would marry (...)[45]

In this case, while the reference to Saint Odo is completely unique in the Inquisition documentation so far studied (and, honestly, given the difficult calligraphy and state of preservation of the document in question, largely a guess), the 'owl's eyes' is a reference found twice in the 1908 issue of the *True Almanac of St. Cyprian*, a periodic publication deriving large portions of its content from the contemporary *Book of St. Cyprian* as well as from various urban folk magic practices,[46] although any relation between these two instances is equally pure conjecture.

If nothing else, what these alternative divination procedures exemplify is the variability of divination practices associated

---

44 Souza, *The Devil and the Land of the Holy Cross*, 95.

45 'pegando em hum aro de peneira, posto hua tisoura, e huã moeda de dez reis, a fazia andar a roda e ella lhe dizia estas palavras: Por virtude de St° Odão(?) S. Ceperião; e Saõ Cepriaõzinho, e os olhos de mocho(?) e mil arvores lhe dissesse se era certo o que lhe que digo(?) [se] era para casar huã Maria Joana', in ANTT, Inquisição de Coimbra, *124° Caderno do Promotor: 2ª Série*, fol.355v.

46 See Leitão, *Opuscula Cypriani*, 849, 851.

with the name of Cyprian, as well as the rich and complex landscape that made up the urban folk magic environment from which the contemporary *Book of St. Cyprian* derives large sections of its content. In this way, the dissociation of the seafaring Cyprian incantation from its original ritual procedure and later association with any other form of divination should not be seen as a particular mystery. Should such have happened through purely organic mechanisms, the creativity of an individual urban folk magic practitioner, or the initiative of the *Book*'s compiler, any of these channels would be equally legitimate within this context.

Removing ourselves from macroscopic observations, one particular trial among the several dealing with Cyprianic hydromancy should be highlighted for demonstrating how such bridges between systems can be constructed; this is the 1729 trial of Domingas Maria.[47] This woman, judging from her record, seems to have been a truly remarkable professional, possessor of a vast and complex arsenal of magical practices (including what is likely to be the only surviving version of the prohibited prayer 'The Testament of Jesus Christ').[48] Of these practices, one can not only find the seafaring Cyprian hydromancy ritual, but also several, albeit fragmented, instances of the use of cartomancy in various rituals. The simplest of these is explicit in mentioning that Domingas and her servant would spread out the cards in a 'certain order which they knew',[49] and a second ritual is described in which she would, firstly, place her cards under 'a disgusting

---

47 See Leitão, *Opuscula Cypriani*, 39-61.

48 Londoño, *Las Oraciones Censuradas*, 17-18.

49 'por certa ordẽ que as mesmas sabiaõ', in ANTT, Inquisição de Lisboa, *Processo nr. 7485*, fol.33r.

vase'[50] (potentially indicating a chamber pot), removing them from there after some time and saying a sequence of mostly imperceivable words, among which that the cards 'should open the door'.[51] While doing this, Domingas would split the cards into three piles and hit them with her hand. In this last instance there isn't any mention of a direct reading of the cards, and this somewhat suggests itself as being in some way a preparatory step for a coscinomancy ritual.

However, her use of cards gains a different relevance when we revisit her seafaring Cyprian hydromancy ritual. In Domingas's case, her particular arrangement of this ritual was one of the two performed with an egg instead of straws, and one where neither virginity nor chastity was invoked, the reading being completely by analogy and not needing any specialized seer. However, in at least one case, having performed this ritual several times for the purpose of knowing if her client's husband was returning from his trip without arriving at any conclusive results, for 'each time the egg was cast it came out different',[52] cartomancy was used to resolve the matter. The cards were taken and shuffled while saying the words:

In the name of the Holiest Trinity discover for me here the whole truth, and in the name of God and the Crucified Christ, open the truth to me;[53]

---

50 'hum vaso imundo', in ANTT, Inquisição de Lisboa, *Processo nr. 7485*, fol.12v.

51 'que lhe abrissem a porta', in ANTT, Inquisição de Lisboa, *Processo nr. 7485*, fol.13r.

52 'de cada vez q̃ se deitava o dito ovo sahiaõ diferentes', in ANTT, Inquisição de Lisboa, *Processo nr. 7485*, fol.76v.

53 'Em nome da Santisima Trindade me descobrias aqui toda a verdade, e em Nome de Deos e de Christo crucificado, me desabras a verdade', in ANTT, Inquisição de Lisboa, *Processo nr. 7485*, fol.76v.

After this, the cards were laid out in five rows, with the name of the missing husband having been given to one of the Kings in the deck. Analyzing the spread, if the King fell on the middle row, then it was a sign that he was returning.

While this ritual is omissive on several points, the parallels between it and the cartomancy systems present in the contemporary *Book* are notable (see Appendix 1A and 1B). Firstly, the mention of the disposition of the cards in five rows could indicate a similar spread to that made with a forty-card deck in five columns of eight cards. Secondly, the significant location of the sought-out card in the middle row is equally reminiscent of the 'novelty' procedure described in the contemporary *Book*, which is prompted when the middle of the five columns does not have any court/figure cards. What is further suggested by this procedure is that, at least for Domingas, there wasn't a fixed and standard significance given to each card. Rather, this was something that should be attributed at the beginning of the ritual to the necessary cards.

This theory seems to be supported by another extremely rare and unique description of the consecration of a deck of cards meant for divination. This is from the 1731 voluntary confession and denunciation of Maria Rosa de Jesus, an apparently well-connected individual in the Lisbon urban folk magic scene, familiar with numerous practitioners:

> She further said that the same woman taught her how to do some lots with a deck of cards in the following way : I conjure thee cards, not as cards, but as ladies, dames, and beautiful, I conjure thee with Barrabás, Satanas, and Cayfas, and Lady Maria de Padilha, with all her gang : which should be said to all cards, one by one, giving each of them its significance and several names, for the above-mentioned purpose, and in order

to know if the mentioned person would come to her house (...)[54]

Even if the card spread and reading is not provided, what this clearly offers is the idea that pre-contemporary urban folk magic cartomancy systems were fluid by nature, being continuously tailored and restructured in accordance with the specificity and details of each individual reading. Most likely, such systems only became stationary in their card significations when they were put down in printed form, meaning that the significations currently given in the contemporary *Book of St. Cyprian* and its several offshoots are merely circumstantial and, in their 'natural habitat', these would be changed and shifted with every single use.

To now address the issue of 'text generation' will require an analysis of a completely distinct system of divination. From among the several dozens of known urban folk magic cases, one system that emerges as being considerably more popular than Cyprianic hydromancy is that of the 'Lots of the Favas', a particular style of favomancy. While a large number of instances and mentions of this divination method have been identified, an extensive and coherent study on all of them is yet to be performed. However, the few instances already analyzed reveal a relative heterogeneity, particularly in terms of its associated incantations. In a general sense, while all these instances do

---

54 'Disse mais, que também a mesma molhér lhe ensinou fizesse huãs sortes com hum baralho de cartas pella forma seguinte : eu te esconjuro cartas, naõ por cartas, màs por senhoras, damas, e galantes, conjurote com Barrabás, Satanas, e Cayfas, e Dona Maria de Padilha, com toda a sua quadrilhá : o que havia de dizer a todas as cartas huã por huma, dando a cada huã dellas sua significaçaõ e diversos nomes, para o sobredito fim, e para saber se a ditta pessoa havia de vir a sua casa', in ANTT, Inquisição de Lisboa, *Processo nr. 10067*, fol.14v.

present very similar elements and a general theme, they can be found in different arrangements and lengths.

According to this favomancy ritual, one should firstly collect an appropriate number of fava beans, most often eighteen. While there is no mention of any particular species or kind of fava, these are sometimes specified as needing to be 'favas de cinco', or five-favas, meaning favas which are found in groups of five in the same pod.[55] These eighteen favas should all be distinguishable from each other, by either being of different colors, different shapes, or having some natural or artificial markings which will make them easily identifiable. Nine of these favas will be identified as being male, and the other nine as female.

After the favas have been acquired they should be consecrated, and the most complete ritual found in the records of the Inquisition mentions this is achieved by baptizing them two times, once 'at home with holy water, which should be taken from church, and then they should once again be baptized in the basin of any church, in the same way in which any creature is baptized, during the feasts of Christmas, Easter, Holy Spirit, and Saint John'.[56] Highlighting the variability and heterogeneity of this process, one report found in a *Caderno* mentions that this baptism should be performed by first walking with the favas through the main gates of a city, taking them to three churches to be dipped in the holy water basin (no incantation is given) and then passing them through three waves of the sea,[57] a step

---

55 ANTT, Inquisição de Lisboa, *Processo nr.247*, fol.8v.

56 'em casa com agoa benta que se havia de ir buscar à Igreja, e depois se havião de tornar a baptisar em huã pia de qualquer Igreja, na forma em que se baptisa huã creatura, nas festas de Natal, Paschoas de Resurreiçaõ, e Spirito Santo,e Saõ João', in ANTT, Inquisição de Lisboa, *Processo nr. 247*, fol.8v-9r.

57 ANTT, Inquisição de Lisboa, *17° Caderno do Promotor*, fol.388v.

reminiscent of the pseudo-hagiographical deck-consecration method present in the contemporary *Book of St. Cyprian*.

Focusing on the more normalized methods, one of the lengthiest baptism incantations is given in the trial of Antónia da Serra (1672) as the following (one variation of this incantation can be consulted in Appendix 4A):

> I conjure thee favas, no more as favas, but as nine men and nine women, baptized with Saint Peter and Saint Paul, with the Apostle Saint James, with the three Missal books, with three Easter candles, with three consecrated Hosts, with perennial fountains, with the Lord who was born in Bethlehem, with Jesus who died in Jerusalem, with the sacred, with the powers of the Holiest Trinity, with three priests invested at the altar giving the three Masses of Christmas, with Saint John of Pauana(?), with the Mother of Our Lady Saint Anne, with the Heavens, with the stars, with the airs, with the winds, with all the elements; as the Lord separated the night from the day, in the same way separate the truth from the lie, as the Lord opened the sea, and path to the children of Israel, in the same way show me in these five lots this that I ask, by the earth in which thou were grown, by the water with which thou

were watered, by the Sun with which thou were dried,
my beloved, and dear, show me the truth in the name
of the three persons of the Holiest Trinity.[58]

Highlighting the close relationship between all the divination
methods so far examined, the preceding incantation, as well as
those present in Appendix 4, bears striking similarities to the
attribution of significations to playing cards in the incantation
of Maria Rosa de Jesus offered above. What is implied in both
instances is the substitution of the nature of the objects in
question, cards or favas, by another, ladies and dames or men
and women, with which one is able to enter into dialogue or
commerce.

Beyond this, the technique of baptism, as used in the
urban folk magic *milieu*, seems to have been one of considerable
versatility, as besides these divinatory instances, yet another
case is known of this same method being used to consecrate
a number of objects and substances used in the creation of an

---

58 'Eu vos esconjuro favas naõ ja por favas, senaõ por nove homẽs
e nove molheres, baptisadas com Saõ Pedro e São Paulo, com o
Apostolo Santigo, com os tres livros missaes, com tres sirios paschoaes,
com tres Hostias consagradas, com fontes perenaes, com o Senhor que
naceo em Betlem, com Jesus que morreo em Jerusalem, com as sacras,
com os poderes da Santissima Trindade com tres Padres revestidos
no altar disendo as tres Missas do Natal, com São João da Pauana(?),
com a May da Senhora Santa Anna, com o Ceo, com as estrellas, com
os ares, com os ventos com todos os elementos, assim como o Senhor
apartou a noite do dia, assim me apartai a verdade da mentira, assim
como o Senhor abrio o mar, e caminho aos filhos de Israel, assim me
mostrai aqui nestas cinco sortes isto que vos peço, pella terra em que
vos criastes, pella agoa com que vos regastes, pello sol com que vos
secastes minhas amadas, e queridas mostraime a verdade em louvor
das tres pessoas da Santissima Trindade', in ANTT, Inquisição de
Lisboa, *Processo nr. 247*, fol.10r.

aspersion. This is from the 1690 trial of Jerónima de Almeida who, probably not coincidently, was herself a cartomancer. While once again fragmented, her card reading system can be noted as being entirely distinct from all those so far analyzed by not utilizing a spread, but rather being a single card draw. This, Jerónima mentioned, she learned from a Castilian woman named Maria de Mello, who used a deck of 'foreign cards'.[59] In this method, a deck should be taken out and cards pulled out of it one by one, while the following words were said at each card: who is it – yes it is – is the lady «naming the client» home – the lord/ladyship is home – what dost thou what from them – this is what I what – this is what I bring – this is what I shall give them – and in this they shall remain.[60] The card taken at the last line (the ninth) would be the one containing the sought answer, and although very little is said about the several card significances, it is mentioned that a King or a Knight (a Jack in a contemporary deck) meant that a man was coming to pick this woman up—if this was of the suit of Diamonds, he would bring money, of Hearts, he would pay with embraces, and of Spades, with heartache.[61]

While there are no mentions of baptizing these cards, this process was still used in order to grant additional virtues to ingredients used in a variety of procedures. Particular among these was a service Jerónima provided in order to increase the fortunes of a store. To do this she would buy several ingredients, there being some confusion over the exact number of them.

---

59 'cartas estrangeiras', in ANTT, Inquisição de Lisboa, *Processo nr. 8465*, fol.15v.

60 'quien és : sin es : esta em caza a senhora fulana, nomeando a pessoa porquem lançava a sorte : em caza está su merce : q̃ lhe quiere hoste : esto le quiero : esto le trago : e esto le ei de dar : j en esto a de quedar', in ANTT, Inquisição de Lisboa, *Processo nr. 8465*, fol.16r.

61 ANTT, Inquisição de Lisboa, *Processo nr. 8465*, fol.16r.

Listed throughout the trial one can find mentions of (male) incense (this can either refer to incense naturally secreted by its plant, or the first incense extract from an individual plant), storax balsam, rosemary, wicks, and flints,[62] as well as French lavender,[63] with the following words being said during this purchase:

> God save thee store stall, storax I come to buy, it is not to hurt, nor kill, it is for Our Lord great fortune give me.[64]

After this, all these objects/ingredients, placed together and tied inside a small cloth, should be baptized in the holy water basin of a church with the words 'I don't baptize a flint, nor storax, nor these trinkets, but rather a pagan child, so as God may give me fortune, and all may come to get me',[65] adding, 'I baptize thee in the name of the Father, the Son, and the Holy Spirit'.[66]

Having finished this ceremony, this cloth should be placed under the consecrator's knee while they attended mass. All these things being done, the baptized objects should be taken to the home/store requesting the service, but the consecrator still needed to exit the church from a different door from the one by

---

62 ANTT, Inquisição de Lisboa, *Processo nr. 8465*, fol.5v.

63 ANTT, Inquisição de Lisboa, *Processo nr. 8465*, fol.8r.

64 'Deos te salve tenda tendal, almeya venho comprar não he para ferir, nem para matar, he para Nosso Senhor muita ventura me dar,' in ANTT, Inquisição de Lisboa, *Processo nr. 8465*, fol.17r.

65 'Eu naõ bautizo isca, nem almea, nem estas nenharias, se naõ hua creança pagã, para q̃ deos me dé ventura e todos me venhaõ buscar', in ANTT, Inquisição de Lisboa, *Processo nr. 8465*, fol.5v-6r; fol.8r.

66 'Eu te baptizo em nome do Padre, do Filho, e do Spirito Santo', in ANTT, Inquisição de Lisboa, *Processo nr. 8465*, fol.6r.

which they entered.[67] Arriving at the ritual location, all ingredients were boiled in holy water taken from three churches belonging to three different parishes (I believe the flint and wick were probably just used to light the fire). This boiling should be stirred with the rosemary branch, while an unregistered incantation was said, and the resulting liquid sprinkled throughout the store with the same branch.[68] Besides this, some of the boiled ingredients, such as the storax balsam, French lavender, and incense, should also be used to fumigate the premises.[69]

Returning to the 'Lots of the Favas', after baptism/ consecration, in order to perform any reading with these favas one must have an accurate understanding of the question or problem at hand so that an appropriate number of male and female favas can be chosen to represent the several male and female individuals involved in the current situation. These favas will need to be baptized once again with the appropriate names, there being a consistent omission from the studied trials as to whether this step should be done with the same incantation as the previous baptism, or by a simpler formula like 'I baptize thee in the name of the Father, the Son, and the Holy Spirit'. Equally, it is unclear whether the double baptism mentioned in the Antónia da Serra trial is somehow alluding to this, meaning that the favas' baptism at church is the only necessary step of their general consecration, and the second baptism mentioned actually refers to this specific and individual baptism which should be performed before a reading, also described as being made using holy water but in one's own home or that of the client. Be this as it may, not all of the favas need to be used in every divination.

---

67 ANTT, Inquisição de Lisboa, *Processo nr. 8465*, fol.8r.

68 ANTT, Inquisição de Lisboa, *Processo nr. 8465*, fol.6r

69 ANTT, Inquisição de Lisboa, *Processo nr. 8465*, fol.18r.

With all the individuals involved being identified, the reader should take the favas representing the two most relevant of these (usually the querent and, for example, her lover/husband/boyfriend, should this be a romantic case, or, in case of theft, the person they are most suspicious about), and hold them both with their teeth. At this point another incantation is said in a soft voice. Given that this step is largely imperceivable to most witnesses to the procedure, only one single instance of this incantation has so far been found, dating from 1648. While its wording is coherent with the remaining known incantations, given its singularity, it is debatable if this is representative of that of other practitioners:

I conjure thee (NN), and (NN) in the name of God the Father, and God the Son and God the Holy Spirit, with the mysteries of the Holiest Trinity, with God born in Bethlehem to the Holy house of Jerusalem, and with the sea, and with the stars, and with the Lord who is among them, with three perennial fountains, and with nine consecrated Hosts, and with nine missal books, and with nine Paschal candles, and with three Christmas masses, with God who parted the night from day, that thou parts the truth from the lies, and with God who opened the paths to the children of Israel,

open the way to these favas to tell me if it is true this
that I ask (...)[70]

The divined upon question should be said immediately after
this incantation, and while the entirety of this procedure is being
done this same single report mentions that the diviner should be
constantly making the sign of the cross over their mouth.

Taking these two favas once again in their hand, the Latin
'hoc este enim corpus meum' should be further said over them.
Afterwards these are mixed together with all the others which
are to be used in this particular reading (it being possible that no
other favas beyond these two are used), as well as a plethora of
other objects and small trinkets, all of which have an associated
significance. Given that these objects and their significances
can be seen to change, not only between trials, but even within
the same trial, it is quite possible that, as in early modern
cartomancy, their selection and associated significance might be
something which should be determined with each new reading.
By surveying a few of these, it is immediately noticeable that their
significations are extremely close, and sometimes even identical,
to those given to the several pip cards in the cartomancy systems
presented in the contemporary *Book of St. Cyprian*, with the favas
taking the place of the court cards. This should not be seen as a
coincidence, but rather the very basis of Portuguese urban folk

---

70 'Eu te coniuro fulano, e fulana em nome de Deos Padre, e de Deos
Filho e Deos Spirito Sancto com os mysterios da Sanctissima Trindade
com Deos nascido em Belem athe a caza Sancta de Heruzalem, e com
o mar, e com as estrelas, e com o Senhor que està entre ellas com tres
fontes perenaes, e com nove hostias consagradas, e com nove livros
missaes, e com nove sirios paschoaes, e com tres missas do Natal, com
Deos que apartiu a noite do dia que apartes as verdades das mintiras,
e com Deos que abrio as carreiras aos filhos de Irrael abra caminho a
estas favas para me dizer é a verdade disto que lhe pergunto (...)', in
ANTT, Inquisição de Lisboa, *30º Caderno do Promotor*, fol.42v-43r.

magic divination, of which the cartomancy systems described in the contemporary *Book* are but one instance.

From the trial of Catarina da Ribeira:[71]

Foreign coin	Money
Piece of paper	Writing/letter
Piece of colored fabric	Dress
Piece of wood	Boat
Piece of jet*	Night
Piece of tile	Marriage
Bread crumb	Eating together
Conch*	Church
Piece of sealing wax	Joy
Piece of wax	Peace
Salt rock	Taste/enjoyment
Piece of alum	Grief
Half a fava	Lying in a bed
Piece of verdigris	Jealousy

*In the trial in question, these are said to be mandatory objects that should be kept/stored together with the favas.

From the trial of Antónia da Serra (Version 1):[72]

Croaker skull bone	Church
Mattress-shaped fabric	Bed
Cloth with black string	Shroud
Piece of flint	Man and woman together

---

71 ANTT, Inquisição de Lisboa, *Processo nr. 11579.*
72 ANTT, Inquisição de Lisboa, *Processo nr. 247.*

Castilian coin	Money
Piece of sulfur	Gold
Piece of sealing wax	Justice
Piece of coral	Joy
Piece of jet	Night
Piece of green ribbon	Person

From the trial of Antónia da Serra (Version 2):

Piece of alum (large)	Grief
Piece of alum (small)	Tears
Piece of sealing wax (large)	War
Piece of sealing wax (small)	Joy
Piece of silk	Gift
Coin	Money
Piece of painted clay	Home/house
Conch (one side)	Laughter
Conch (the other side)	Sea
Piece of stitched linen	Bed
Piece of flint	Man and woman together

Besides these, other objects mentioned but not given a significance are a variety of coins, different fabrics, colored stones or pieces of ceramic, a black medal,[73] dice,[74] date pits, and a piece of gold.[75]

Thus put together, all these objects are mixed, being passed from one hand of the reader to the other until one further

---

73 ANTT, Inquisição de Lisboa, *Processo nr. 11579*, fol.23v.

74 ANTT, Inquisição de Lisboa, *Processo nr. 247*, fol.14v.

75 ANTT, Inquisição de Lisboa, *Processo nr. 12722*, fol.3v.

incantation is said, with the reader's mouth over them (further alternatives to this incantation can be consulted in Appendix 4B):

> With Saint Peter, and Saint Paul, with the Lord who was born in Bethlehem, with Jesus who died in Jerusalem, with three Priests revested at the altar, giving the three Masses of Christmas, with the sacred, with the powers of the Holiest Trinity; and as the Lord opened the path to the children of Israel, show me here what I wish to know, by the earth which grew thee, by the water which watered thee, by the Sun which dried thee, paint me the truth in these three lots in the name of the Holiest Trinity.[76]

Finally, everything is cast over a surface and, by analyzing the relative positions of the several favas among themselves, and their respective proximity or distance from the other objects, the reader constructs a narrative involving all the individuals named and the various events detailed by the objects. The incantation further suggests that this casting should performed several times (three in the above instance), but no mentions have been found of how these successive castings function or communicate with each other. As a last detail, according to one single trial,

---

76 'Com Saõ Pedro, e com Saõ Paulo, com o Senhor que nasceo em Belem, com Jesus que morreo em Jerusalem, com tres Padres revestidos no altar dizendo as tres Missas do Natal, com as sacras, com os poderes da Santissima Trindade, e assim como o Senhor abrio o caminho aos filhos de Israel assim me mostrai aqui o que pertendo saber pella terra em que vos creastes, pella agoa com que vos regastes, p^{lo} sol com que vos secastes, que me pinteis a verdade nestas tres sortes em louvor da Santissima Trindade', in ANTT, Inquisição de Lisboa, *Processo nr. 247*, fol.27r.

this divination method should only be used on Mondays and Wednesdays.

Thus looking back upon the cartomancy systems presented in the *Book of St. Cyprian*, and their innovative 'text generation', it becomes obvious that there is nothing novel about this. The only novelty that the *Book*'s cartomancy systems offer is simply that of a more structured, or strictly linear text generation; the cards are read in a predetermined order, while the favas will always offer an unpredictable and unsystematizable disposition.

CONCLUSIONS

The contemporary *Book of St. Cyprian*, as one of its most relevant points, presents three sections detailing two different systems of cartomancy. One of these in particular presents an unusual incantation which seems out of place in relation to this system's symbolism and ritual procedure. This same incantation is also found in a few brief mentions in other nineteenth-century *Books of St. Cyprian*, as well as folk magic divinatory techniques, indicating that its origin is not only external to the printed nineteenth-century *Books*, but probably much older than them.

Knowing that some of the content of the *Book of St. Cyprian* can be traced to a particular magic style found in Iberian and South American urban centers throughout the early modern period, it is noticeable that incantations similar to the one associated with cartomancy in the contemporary *Book* can also be found among those early modern magical practices. However, in that environment the incantations were consistently associated with hydromancy, Saint Cyprian's main realm of action within that magic style.

Analysis of these incantations reveals that all their individual elements and symbols refer to concrete objects and actions one is meant to enact during their associated hydromancy ritual. While there is still a lack of middle steps in the sequence of historical transmission between these hydromancy rituals and the contemporary Cyprian cartomancy systems, what is suggested is that, while hydromancy fell out of use in favor of cartomancy in urban magical circles, Cyprian's realm of action within urban folk magic did not shift significantly, and he simply became the patron of a newly favored divinatory system, and with this transfer of domain also came his previous incantation, which maintained its previous hydromancy symbolism and references.

Furthermore, at least one urban folk magic practitioner is known to have associated Cyprianic hydromancy with cartomancy, using a card layout reminiscent of one of those present in the contemporary *Book*, as well as a simple system of free and specifically tailored associations between cards and significations. Further investigation into cartomancy in this same magical environment suggests that, in this form of divinatory practice, this was the proper way of working with playing cards; with each new spread or question being divined, each card would need to be given a new significance in accordance with the specific circumstances involved. This suggests that the card significations present in the *Book* are merely circumstantial and should in fact be changed and tailored for each unique reading.

As another aspect of the cartomancy systems present in the contemporary *Book*, the reading of their several card spreads acts as a form of narrative or 'text generation', this being a rather unique and specialized aspect of these systems. Still, continuous exploration of the various techniques present in early modern urban folk magic reveals that this same form of 'text generation' is common, and mostly associated with favomancy. In this, much like in early modern Portuguese cartomancy, a variable number of favas and other objects are given variable and tailorable significances and associations, with their casting generating a kind of 'map' of relationships, which should be read through the creation of a narrative.

With all of this, the cartomancy systems present in the contemporary *Book of St. Cyprian* reveal themselves as a combinatory arrangement of an array of principles, general ideas, and techniques utilized in several divinatory methodologies associated with Portuguese urban folk magic. None of their different elements are unique or novel in themselves, only their particular combination presented in the contemporary *Book*. We have thus solved the origin of the seafaring Cyprian incantation, the problematic card significations presented in the contemporary *Book*, and the apparent uniqueness of these systems' manner of 'text generation' (or at least pushed these questions back four hundred years).

Finally, as an ever-important concluding remark, this is not to say that the cartomancy systems presented in the contemporary *Book of St. Cyprian* are an inferior pastiche or derivative system, or a corruption of older or more complex divinatory methods. To claim such a thing is to simply not understand history. The point of this monograph is not to demonstrate the fraudulent or false nature of any system by placing it before its 'pure' ancestors (which would be a fall into the 'archaic' fallacy), it is simply to give it back its history. The several Cyprian cartomancy systems that have sprung up since the nineteenth century are the current expressions of a multi-century tradition of urban folk divination; they are not its usurpers, they are its saviors and children. They are what remained, what survived, and what moved forward in a world of constantly changing habits and mentalities. Cyprian cartomancy is the new meat currently dressing the bones of Portuguese urban divination.

Appendix 1A: 'System of casting cards'

from the contemporary *Book of St. Cyprian*

Anon., *O Grande Livro de S. Cypriano*, part 1, 73-78; Leitão, *The Book of St. Cyprian*, 48-52.

System of casting cards

Cartomancy, or the divination through playing cards, is more modern, for cards were only invented after Charles V. This branch of the conjectural sciences, still today practiced by many people, and sincerely accredited by many more, is the great resource of lovesick girls, using it out of jealousy, suspicion and longing for the object of their affections. Cartomancy is practiced with thirty-two cards, or with a deck of seventy-eight. Today, among us, the forty card deck will be used, with each card meaning one of the things we will thus expose:

DIAMONDS

The *Ace* – a gift
The *Two* – soon
The *Three* – with joy
The *Four* – church
The *Five* – novelty
The *Six* – meager money
The *Seven* – much money

SPADES

The *Ace* – affirmation/statement
The *Two* – cutting
The *Three* – bad words
The *Four* – in bed
The *Five* – sickness
The *Six* – detour/deviation
The *Seven* – passion of the soul

HEARTS

The *Ace* – a ball/dance/party
The *Two* – a letter
The *Three* – good words
The *Four* – placed in the front of the exit door
The *Five* – tears
The *Six* – through paths
The *Seven* – at eating or drinking time

CLUBS

The *Ace* – by night
The *Two* – through long paths
The *Three* – through fast paths
The *Four* – in this house
The *Five* – with the five senses
The *Six* – zeal
The *Seven* – with great pleasure

The queen of spades is a bad talking woman, and the king and jack of spades are the body and mind of a man connected with justice, be him a lawyer, a judge, a prosecutor or anything of the sort.

The queen of diamonds represents the sorceress' consultant, the king and jack of diamonds the body and mind of the consultant or the individual one desires to know something about.

All other figures are used to represent people who might play a part of this nigromancy, being obvious that the jacks represent the thought of the individuals marked by the kings of the same suit.

The disposition of the cards, after being shuffled and cross-cut, which should be accompanied by words in which one places great importance and with which one asks St. Cyprian to reveal the intended answer through the cards, should be made as thus:

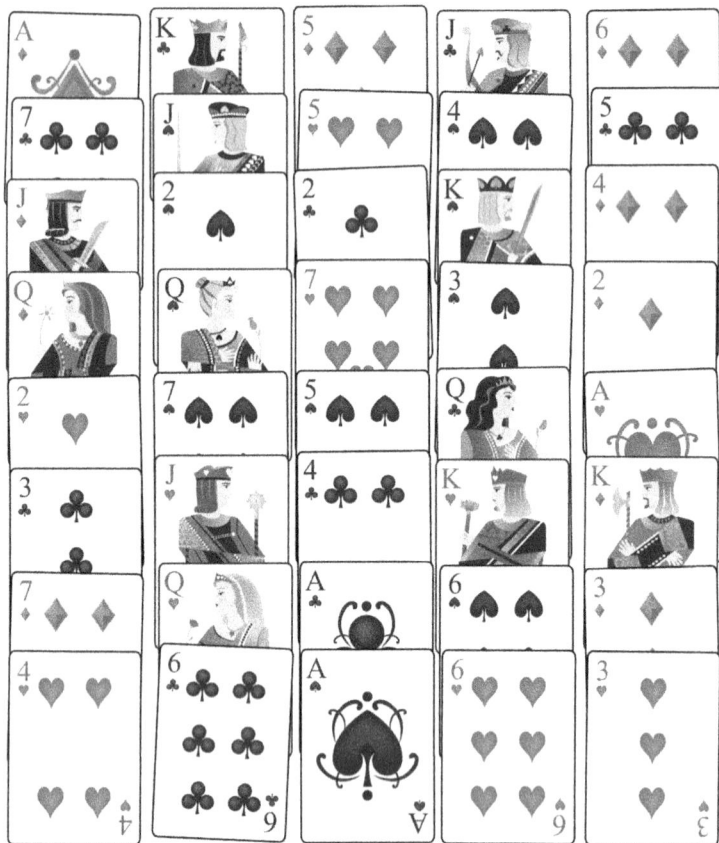

Let us suppose that it is a girl in love who is consulting the sorceress, and that the cards were drawn as the figure demonstrates. The sorceress, starting by the Three of Hearts and the Ace of Diamonds, across from each other, would say:

"Good words with a gift, with joy and great pleasure, this man, of body and soul is with this woman and with a ball…"

Holy name of Jesus! The good old lady has divined a terrible secret, such a secret that it makes her consultant faint, for she would never imagine that a card could reveal the loss of her innocence, taken while hiding from prying eyes…

The old woman, sprinkling some cold water on the pale cheeks of her customer, continues with her nigromancy…

"Soon, with the church through fast paths…" (the girl will be married very soon, for I drew here the figure of the church with great haste…) "With five senses with much money and meager money, through the exit door…, etc., etc."

She may then continue with great volubility, always drawing *crossed* cards from the next two *columns* and on to the center.

"We have a *novelty*, for the middle column does not have any figures. Let us see then. What does thou wish for me to look for in this *novelty*?"

"What I wish to know is if he is faithful to me."

"Very well. The *novelty* will tell."

The sorceress whispers in a low voice:

Pt: "Cartas, pelo poder de S. Cypriano, que sete annos no mar andou, e sete sortes por sua divina esposa deitou, dizei-me se este senhor guarda fé e lealdade a esta senhora. Se lhe é fiel saia elle com ella com muito gosto, mas se é infiel saia com outra mulher, tendo *desvio* d'esta senhora."

En: "Cards, by the power of St. Cyprian, who seven years the sea roamed, and seven lucks for his divine wife he cast, tell me if this man is keeping himself faithful and loyal to this woman. If he is faithful, let him go out with her with great pleasure, but if he is unfaithful, let him go out with some other woman, having been *diverted* from this one."

You then place 21 cards facing down over the middle *column* and you place by the side of this column 8 cards, two by two in a *cross*, so as you will end up with only three cards in your hand. If these three cards *do not tell you anything* start drawing from the 8 at the side, in a cross from each other, and read what they say, then go to the column of 21, taking one from one extremity of the column and one from the other until you run out of cards. If such is the case that you cannot satisfy the curiosity of the girl, you must bend the significance of two or three cards, making them fit to the best of your abilities to what she wishes to know, and thus your job is done,

One must also take note that should the Four of Diamonds be drawn with the Four or Five of Spades that this is the signal of death soon to come.

The Two of Hearts with the Four of Diamonds indicates a marriage.

Appendix 1B: 'Way of reading the cards exactly like St. Cyprian did'

from the contemporary *Book of St. Cyprian*

Anon., *O Grande Livro de S. Cypriano*, part 1, 87-93; Leitão, *The Book of St. Cyprian*, 60-63.

Way of reading the cards exactly like St. Cyprian did

THE MEANING OF THE CARDS

DIAMONDS

The *Ace*, a gift
The *Two*, soon
The *Three*, with joy
The *Four*, church
The *Five*, novelty
The *Six*, meager money
The *Seven*, much money

SPADES

The *Ace*, affirmation/statement
The *Two*, cutting
The *Three*, bad words
The *Four*, in bed
The *Five*, sickness
The *Six*, detour/deviation
The *Seven*, passion of the soul

HEARTS

The *Ace*, a ball/dance/party
The *Two*, a letter
The *Three*, good words
The *Four*, placed in the front of the exit door
The *Five*, tears
The *Six*, through paths
The *Seven*, at eating or drinking time

CLUBS

The *Ace*, by night
The *Two*, through long paths
The *Three*, through fast paths
The *Four*, in this house
The *Five*, with the five senses
The *Six*, zeal
The *Seven*, with great pleasure

So as to know how to read what the cards reveal to the consultant

The *queen of spades* is a woman of ill fame or of a bad sign. The *king* and *jack of spades* are the body and thoughts of a man of justice. If a woman is consulting the cards she should be represented by the *queen of diamonds*, and the *king* and *jack* of this same suit represent the position and thought of the individual who the consultant wishes to know about. Should it be a man he should be represented by the *king* and *jack of diamonds*, and the person consulted about should be represented by the *queen* of this same suit. All other figures are used to mark any other person who might be mentioned in this nigromancy, knowing that the *jacks* represent thoughts of the individuals marked by the *kings* of the same suit.

THE WAY OF DISPLAYING THE CARDS

After the cards are shuffled and cut into a cross, divided into five equal portions and placed into rows of three piles, making like this a cross, and all this operation should be accompanied by the responsory, just as St. Cyprian did, so as the cards do not fail in their response to you.

Let us suppose that it is an infatuated girl who is consulting the cards, and these, after shuffled and spread on the table, are as follows:

1st line – Ace of diamonds, 7 of clubs, jack of diamonds, queen of diamonds, ace of hearts, 2 of clubs, 5 of diamonds and 4 of spades.

2nd line – King of clubs, jack of spades, 2 of spades, king of spades, 7 of spades, queen of hearts, king of hearts and 6 of clubs.

3rd line – 5 of diamonds, 5 of hearts, 2 of clubs, 7 of hearts, 5 of spades, 4 of clubs, ace of clubs and ace of spades.

4th line – jack of clubs, 4 of spades, king of spades, 3 of spades, queen of clubs, king of hearts, 6 of spades and 6 of hearts

5th line – 6 of diamonds, 6 of clubs, 4 of diamonds, 2 of diamonds, ace of hearts, king of diamonds, 3 of diamonds and 3 of hearts.

If the cards come out as we have just described you should read them as follows; but, if they do not, you should study their meaning, for without knowing this you will not extract any benefit from them.

We now start from the cards on the columns by the sides, across from each other, by the *three of hearts* and the *ace of diamonds*, and, consulting their meaning, you can see that they mean these words: *a gift with great joy and a night of pleasure.* "This man with his thought on this woman and with ideas for her, with a paper for church by quick paths, with five senses in much money and meager money, coming by the exit door."

It is then obvious that she is to be married quite soon with the individual about whom she inquired, with a great fortune arising from this consortium, having still to accept a gift from him before all this comes to pass. We then begin this same operation with the next lines, extracting from them their meaning. Arriving at the middle column we see that there is a *novelty*, for it has no figures; when this happens we may ask this *novelty* anything we wish, for example: the consulting girl wishes to know if the person she loves is faithful to her; you then take the 32 cards which were already consulted and reshuffle them.

After this, keep the cards in your hand until you finish the responsory of St. Cyprian; after you have finished this, place 21 cards, facing down, over the 8 of the middle column, and place, next to this column, 8 cards, two by two, in a cross, in such a way that you are left with 3 cards in your hand; if these 3 do not tell you anything, start by the 8 by the sides in a cross and read what they say; after this pass to the 21, taking one from each extremity of the column until you are done. One should know that the 4 of diamonds, or the 5 of spades, is a sign of an imminent death and the 2 of hearts with the 4 of diamonds, is an omen of joy, which the person involved will soon discover.

We know that there are many people who cast cards, but of what good is this if they do not possess the *Great Book of St. Cyprian or the Sorcerer's Treasure*, to study and memorize the responsory that one must say, just as the Saint used to say?

Here is how St. Cyprian invented this method: This Saint, after repenting the evil life he led, left his motherland and went to a faraway place and there he remained for seven years. As this Saint had a great deal of love for his wife and children, and also did not have any news from his parents, he decided to develop this system. He used to say: "Back when I was the lord of Satan's cunnings, I cast the cards by the power of my lord, who was Lucifer, however, now I know not how to do this."

He remained meditative on this issue, retiring to his bed at night. There, an Angel of the Lord appeared to him and said, "Cyprian, on what art thou thinking? Hast, by any chance, that cursed one thou abandoned greater power than thy God, who rules over everything illuminated by the Sun? Is thy faith still not true?" after which the angel left.

St. Cyprian woke and said, "This night I had the most pleasant dream; for who has more power than God? I still remember the day when I made fire rain from the Sky over the Earth by the power of Lucifer.

"And a single woman, just by saying – Jesus! – made all the fire cease. Great is the power of Our Lord Jesus Christ!"

Thinking of these things he said, "I shall then cast the cards in the name of Our Lord Jesus Christ," and so he did.

St. Cyprian endowed the cards with great virtues, so as they could divine all that he desired; as such, all those who do not do as this will not reap any benefit from the cards. If they do so this is a sign of imposture.

Cyprian took the deck of cards and passed them, one by one, in seven basins of holy water, each one from its own church; after this he said the Creed over them in a cross, that is, made the sign of the cross over them with his right hand. Next he passed them through the waves of the sea, wrapped seven times so as not to get them wet.

After this the cards could divine all that was happening with his family and all other things he desired.

RESPONSORY THAT SHOULD BE SAID BEFORE CASTING THE CARDS

Pt: Ó meu amantissimo Senhor, vós que sois Deus do universo, permitti que estas cartas me declarem o que eu quero saber, porque, Senhor, não tenho mais a pedir; o senhor seja commigo e me ajude e me soccorra; Maria Santissima, minha mãe, soccorrei-me por intervenção de vosso amado Filho. Senhor meu, a quem com uma vivissima fé, amo de todo o meu coração, corpo, alma e vida. Cartas, vós não me haveis de faltar a isto pelo sangue derramado de Nosso Senhor Jesus Christo. Amen.

En: Oh my most beloved Lord, Thou, who art the God of the Universe, allow that these cards tell me what I wish to know, for, Lord, I have no one else to whom I may ask: the Lord be with me and aid me and save me. Holiest Mary, my mother, save me by intervention of Thy beloved Son, my Lord, whom I love with a most vivid faith with all my heart, and body, and soul, and life; cards, thou shall not fail me, this by the blood Our Lord Jesus Christ shed. Amen.

This is the way to cast the cards; those that do not do as such will not obtain good results.

Appendix 1C: 'Crossed Cartomancy'

from the contemporary *Book of St. Cyprian*

Anon., *O Grande Livro de S. Cypriano*, part 2, 101-111; Leitão,
The Book of St. Cyprian, 135-142.

CROSSED CARTOMANCY

Method of casting the cards, unknown still to this day, and used by St. Cyprian

In the miserable cell which housed St. Cyprian, his last residence
before his death, and hidden in the empty space where he used
to sleep, a manuscript was found with this new art of card
reading that we have named *crossed cartomancy*, of which Cyprian
made use of after his dealings with Satan went sour.

Many years after the death of St. Cyprian, this manuscript
was discovered and taken to Rome, where it was condemned to
be burned after experimentations on its authority in divination
were performed. Such was the effectiveness they found in it
that, fearful, they wished to destroy it by fire.

Gladly this did not to come to pass, maybe due to the will of
the Saint, whose soul had already taken flight to join the Lord.
The one in charge of destroying the manuscript substituted it
with another one, which he threw into the fire under the sight
of all those surrounding him, saving the real one. Later this
manuscript appeared in the Library of Rome, being that it is
still a mystery as to who actually left it there. It is thought that it
was indeed its original keeper or his relatives. But nothing can
be known for sure. That it is authentic is without a doubt, for
with it was also found the order of its condemnation. Due to

the amiability of a friend, who recently visited the Holy City, and whose curiosity took him to the library where this precious manuscript resides, which he then copied, we can, in this edition of the *Great Book of Saint Cyprian*, teach it to the reader.

The deck, composed of 40 cards, should have been passed by the waves of the sea, at midday on a Friday, while uttering at that time the following words:

Pt: Que os espiritos celestes vos ponham a virtude.

En: May the celestial spirits give thee the virtue.

Value of the Cards

Diamonds

Ace – Promise
Two – Marriage
Three – Cuddles of love
Four – Separation
Five – Seduction
Six – Meager fortune
Seven – Wealth

Spades

Ace – Passion
Two – Correspondence
Three – Loyalty
Four – In the house
Five – Plot
Six – Brevity
Seven – Heartbreak

Hearts

Ace – Constraints
Two – Reconciliation
Three – Sympathy
Four – Banquette
Five – Jealousy
Six – Delay
Seven – Surprise

Clubs

Ace – Vice
Two – Treason
Three – Disorder
Four – Levity
Five – Out of the house
Six – Captivity
Seven – Obstacle

The *aces* and the *sevens* also have the special name of *Temptations*.

FIGURES

There are four indispensable figures: the *queen of diamonds*, which represents the consultant; the *king of diamonds*, her boyfriend (or husband); the *queen of spades*, a rival; and the *jack of hearts*, an intermediary person, who can either be a man or a woman.

The remaining figures are only useful when you need to represent other people, who the consultant may suspect.

Any *queen* should be indicated by the words: *this woman*, and a *king* or a *jack* by the words: *this man*, except the *jack of hearts*, which should be named: *this person*.

One should understand that it is necessary to switch the figures if it is a man making the consultation. That is, the consultant should be represented by the *king of diamonds*, the lover (or wife) by the *queen of diamonds*; the *jack of spades* will be a rival and the *jack of hearts* is not substituted for it merely represents an intermediate person, with no definition of gender.

We then usually only have 4 figures, which, with the remaining 28 cards, make up 32; but, in this case, we only cast 24, as was indicated by the Saint.

Firstly remove the *figures* you will not be using.

Then, separate the *aces* and the *sevens* and shuffle these eight cards together (these are the *temptation*), placing them in a pile, in the middle of the table, facing down.

We then have 24 cards in our hand.

Next, shuffle these 24 cards, and cast them over the table, facing up in the form of a cross, whose middle is the pile of the *temptation*:

Start in this order:

One should have the greatest care in observing what we indicate here, so as this consultation may be of some use.

Then continue until you have placed the rest of the cards over the previous ones, in piles of three, as indicates the following figure:

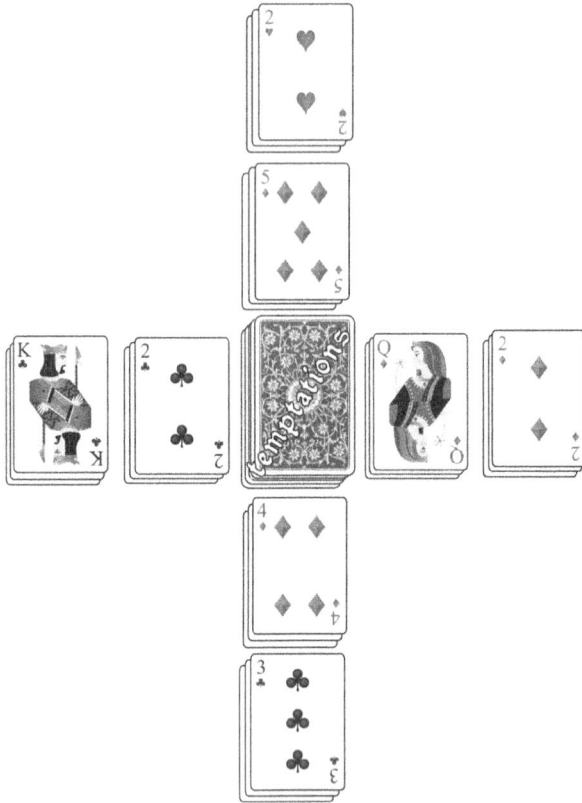

On this occasion, at last, everything is ready to begin uncovering the secrets of the *crossed cartomancy*. And thus, by raising your eyes, placing your thoughts in Heaven and seeking to become possessed by the greatest of faiths, extend your hands over the center of the table, praying in a low and soft voice the following orison of St. Cyprian, which should also be repeated every time one shuffles the cards:

Pt: Que estas cartas, pelo poder de S. Cypriano, hoje Santo e outr'ora feiticeiro, digam a verdade, para gloria do mesmo Santo e satisfação da minha alma.

En: May these cards, by the power of St. Cyprian, now a saint and previously a sorcerer, tell me the truth, for the glory of this same saint and the satisfaction of my soul.

As soon as one has cast the first eight cards, cross yourself with the remaining, saying:

Pt: S. Cypriano seja commigo.

En: St. Cyprian with me.

These four words should be accompanied, respectively, with the movements of your hand, that is, taking your hand to your forehead, one should say: *Saint* – by placing your hand on your chest say: *Cyprian* – with your hand on your left shoulder say: *with* – and, with your hand on you right shoulder to finish – *me*.

Then cast the second group of eight cards and cross yourself with the remaining, repeating the same words. Finally, as should be obvious, conclude with the last cards.

We believe we have explained as clearly as possible the ceremony and the order in which the cards should be cast, so as they end up as the figure demonstrates.

The *crossed cartomancy* may be applied for the uncovering of any mystery; for one needs only to personify the cards with the names of people one assumes to take part in what he wishes to know.

To uncover the cards one follows a different order. Starting by turning one card from each extreme of the cross, continuing to the next extreme, and, as soon as all eight have been lifted, draw one *temptation*. Meaning, turn them in the following order:

Very rarely will one need to lift every card, for, usually, the first nine cards alone should be enough to satisfy the curiosity of the consultant. But, if there remains any desire to know something else, keep going until the next stop in a *temptation*.

When you have lifted all the cards and their meaning has become confusing do the following:

Reshuffle the temptations, place them back in their place, shuffle the rest of the cards and, at last, proceed to a new operation, everything as in the beginning.

FINAL WARNING

The *three of diamonds* (*cuddles of love*) may mean *care* and *affection*, or even a *gift*; the *ace of hearts* (*constraints*) may, at times, mean *violence* (a raped woman, for example); the *two of spades* (*correspondence*) may represent a letter; and the *ace of clubs* (*captivity*) means *imprisoned by love*, or it may represent prison as in actual jail, all according to the circumstances of the consultation.

APPENDIX 2A: KNOWN SAINT CYPRIAN HYDROMANCY REFERENCES WITH COMPLETE INCANTATIONS AND RITUAL PROCEEDINGS

1624: Lisbon Inquisition, 4ᵗʰ Prosecutor's Notebook, fol.702r-702v.

Pt: (…) tomando hũ ourinol cheo d'agua com nove palhinhas dentro, e hũa candeia accesa junto á elle hũa donzela, e se chamasse maria melhor dizendo ahy as palavras seguintes – Bemaventurado San Cipriano as vossas nove sortes no mar as deitastes, se bẽ as deitastes melhor as appanhastes polla vossa santidade, e polla minha virgindade que me mostreis nestas aguas claras, e alvas meu paé (ou a pessoa ausente, de que se deseja saber) se tẽ saude – e que se o santo quisesse mostrar no ourinol o veria (…)

En: (…) taking a chamber pot full of water with nine straws inside, and a lit lamp [and] near it a damsel, and if this was called Maria so much the better, saying the following words – Blessed Saint Cyprian, thy nine lots in the sea thou cast, if good thou cast them, better thou took them, by thy sanctity, and by my virginity show me in these clear and white waters if my father (or the absent person of which one wishes to know of) is of health – and if the saint wished to show this she would see it in the chamber pot (…)

1624: Lisbon Inquisition, 7th Prosecutor's Notebook, fol.508r-508v.

Pt: (…) hera tomar hum ourinol e enchello dagoa até cima, e por junto delle hũa candea aceza, e nove palhinhas as quais hia deitando hũa, e hũa nagoa q̃ estava dentro do ditto orinol fazendo hũa cruz cõ cada hũa dellas na boca do orinol, e emquanto a fazia dizia as palavras seguintes – Bem aventurado Saõ Cepriano nove sortes no mar deitastes assim como a deitastes assim as apanhastes pella vossa santidade, e pela minha virgindade me mostrai aqui meu pay, e entaõ se punha com a cabessa baixa a ver no fundo do ourinol se lhe representava hũa figura como vestida de negro, e assentado, e por ahy emtendeo q̃ o ditto seu padrasto era vivo (…)

En: (…) this was to take a chamber pot and fill it with water to the top, and placing near it a lit lamp, and nine straws, which she would drop, one by one, in the water inside the mentioned chamber pot, making a cross with each of them over the mouth of the chamber pot, while saying the following words – Blessed Saint Cyprian, nine lots in the sea thou cast, as thou cast them, so thou took them, by thy sanctity, and by my virginity, show me here my father, and then she would put her head low, seeing if at the bottom of the chamber pot a figure dressed in black, and seated, would be presented to her, and by this she understood that her stepfather was alive (…)

1624: Lisbon Inquisition, 7ᵗʰ Prosecutor's Notebook, fol.516r.

Pt: (…) enchendo hũ ourinol dagua, e pondo lhe nove palhinhas, e hũa candeinha de sera aceza ay junto, e dizendo bem aventurado Saõ Sepriano as vossas sortes mal as deitastes e se mal as deitastes melhor as tirastes, e loguo falou hũas palavras (?) q̃ dizia q̃ era a confissaõ he pecadora mtº errada e entoã dizia pella vossa sanctidade, e pella minha virgindade me mostrais aqui se he vivo se morto Joaõ primo della teste. (…)

En: (…) filling a chamber pot with water, and putting in it nine straws, and a lit wax lamp close by, and saying, blessed Saint Cyprian, thy lots thou cast them bad, if thou cast them bad, better thou took them, and then she said some words (…) which she said was the confessions, and she was a greatly misled sinner, and then she said, by thy sanctity, and by my virginity, show me here if João, cousin of her the witness, is dead or alive (…)

1625: Lisbon Inquisition, 7ᵗʰ Prosecutor's Notebook, fol.346v.

Pt: (…) deitando em hum ourinol cheo de aguoa a ditta Francisca Lopez nove palhas dizendo quando deitava cada huã as palavras seguintes – Senhor Sam Sypriano bispo e arcebispo confessor de meu Senhor Jesus Xpõ vos pello mar andastes nove sortes no mar as deitastes se boas as deitastes milhores as apanhastes pessovos sancto bendito pella vossa sanctidade e pella vergindade desta menina (falando da ditta Mariana) que vos nos mostreis nestas aguoas claras e auvas tudo aquillo que vos perguntado e verdade for (?) todas tres a saber Barbara Ferram e Francisca Lopez e Maria de Saa deziaõ queremos saber esta moça onde esta ou tal cousa ou tal o que ellas queriaõ saber e loguo se punhaõ a olhar no ourinol (…)

En: (…) the mentioned Francisca Lopes, casting nine straws into a chamber pot filled with water was saying, when casting each one, the following words – Lord Saint Cyprian, bishop and archbishop, confessor of my Lord Jesus Christ, through the sea thou roamed, nine lots in the sea thou cast, if good thou cast them, better thou picked them, I ask thee blessed saint, by thy sanctity, and by the virginity of this girl (speaking of the mentioned Mariana) that thou show us in these clear and white waters all which may be asked and may be true (?) all three, meaning Barbara Ferrão, Francisca Lopes and Maria de Sá would say, we want to know where this girl is, or this or that, that they wanted to know, and immediately they would be staring into the chamber pot (…)

1640: Lisbon Inquisition, 19th Prosecutor's Notebook, fol.147v.

Pt: (…) tomou ella confitente hum ourinol e lhe deitou huã pouca de augua e lancou na dita augua dentro do dito ourinol nove palhinhas que fez de um iunco todas do tamanho de hum alfinete e a cada huã que lancava hia dizendo as palavras seguintes, bem avinturado Saõ Sepriano as vosas sortes no mar deitastes se bem as deitastes milhor as tirastes pecovos pella vossa santidade pella minha vergindade que nesta sorte descubri esta verdade se Pedro de Saõ Martinho he morto ou vivo apareça aqui as quais palavras hia a dita menina repetindo assi como ella confitente lhas hia ensinado (…)

En: (...) she the confessant took a chamber pot and cast some water into it, and in the said water in the said chamber pot she cast nine straws, which she made from a reed, all of the size of needles, and to each that she would cast she would say the following words, blessed Saint Cyprian, thy lots in the sea thou cast, if good thou cast them, better thou took them, I ask thee, by thy sanctity, by my virginity, that in these lots thou discover this truth, if Pedro de São Martinho is dead or alive may he appear here, which words the mentioned girl would repeat as she the confessant would be teaching her (...)

1648: Lisbon Inquisition, Trial nr. 9667, fol.5v, fol.9r.

Pt: (...) tomava hum orinol cõ agoa e lançando lhe dentro nove palhas cada huã por sua vez, e rezando hum padre nosso e huã ave maria e hum credo em cada palha que lançava e dizendo depois : Bem aventurado Saõ Cypriano as ondas do mar passastes, as vossas sortes deitastes, se bem as deitastes, melhor as apanhastes, pella vossa sanctidade, e pella minha castidade me mostreis nestas agoas claras, se há de cazar dom Joaõ com D. Anna (...)

(...) lançava (?) hum orinol cheo de agoa nove palhas dizendo a cada huã que lançava: Bem aventurado Saõ Cypriano, as vossas sortes no mar as deitastes, se bem as deitastes, melhor as apanhastes, pella vossa santidade e pella minha virgindade me mostrai nestas agoa claras se dom Joaõ há de cazar com d. Anna e a as dittas palavras insinava a ditta Maria da Cunha (...) repetindo em o fim dellas digo(?) a cada huã das dittas palhas hum padre nosso, Ave maria, e credo (...)

En: (...) she would take a chamber pot with water and casting into this nine straws, each by its own turn, and praying an Our

Father, and a Hail Mary and a Creed at each straw she cast, saying afterwards: Blessed Saint Cyprian, the waves of the sea thou crossed, thy lots thou cast, if good thou cast them, better thou picked them, by thy sanctity, and by my virginity, show me in these clear waters, if D. João shall marry Lady Ana (…)

(…) she cast (?) into a chamber pot filled with water nine straws, saying at each one she cast: Blessed Saint Cyprian, thy lots in the sea thou cast, if good thou cast them, better thou picked them, by thy sanctity, and by my virginity, show me in these clear waters if D. João shall marry Lady Ana, and the mentioned words the mentioned Maria da Cunha would teach (…) repeating at the end of them, rather, at each of the straws an Our Father, Hail Mary and Creed (…)

1657: Lisbon Inquisition, 37th Prosecutor's Notebook, fol.532r-532v, fol.533r.

Pt: (…) tomando hũ pocaro com agua lançaraõ dentro delle huns junquinhos, e depois diceraõ huas palavras e estas palavras as diceraõ M[a] d[te] e Clemencia sobreditas, ou ambas juntam[te] ou cada huã por si. e a forma das palavras he || S. Cypriano Bpo, e Arcebpo de meu Sr Jesu christo, q̃ as sete sortes, ou as sortes no mar botastes, se as bem botastes melhor as achastes pella vossa sanctidade, e pella minha virgindade me mostrai aqui o q̃ he feito de Sebastiam lousado. | | E depois disto olharaõ dentro do pucaro, e diceraõ q̃ viraõ huãs somas como homens. E declarou ella denunciante q̃ ella mesma pedio às duas sobreditas q̃ lançassem as sortes. E declarou mais, q̃ ella se retirou p[a] outra casa no tempo e acto, q̃ se lançaraõ, e q̃ huã das q̃ se acharoã presentes lhe disse, q̃ ao púcaro, e junquinhos ajuntaraõ mais huã thesoura em cruz (…)

(...) lançaraõ huãs sortes q̃ disem as sortes de S. Cypriano.
E o modo dellas foi, q̃ tendo hũ pucaro de vidro cheo de agoa
tomaraõ sete junquinhos iguais de comprimto da largura de
hũ dedo, e disendo estas palavras; ‖ Bemavaneturado Sam
Cypriano, q̃ as sete sortes no mar botastes, se bem as botastes
melhor as achastes, pella vossa sanctidade e pella minha virgind^e,
q̃ me mostreis q̃ he feito de fulano, se he morto se he vivo ‖ E
acabadas estas palavras lançavaõ hũ dos sete junquinhos dentro
do pucaro, e resevaõ hũ credo, e assim as foraõ repetindo sete
veses. E no fim olharaõ p^a dentro do pucaro e ella denunciante
naõ vio nada.

En: (...) taking a pot with water they cast into it some little
reeds, and then said some words, and these words were said
by the mentioned Maria Duarte and Clemencia, or both of
them together, or each one by herself. And the words were ‖
Saint Cyprian, Bishop and Archbishop of my Lord Jesus Christ,
who thy seven lots, or lots, in the sea thou cast, if good thou
cast them, better thou found them, by thy sanctity, and by my
virginity, show me here what is made of Sebastião Lousado ‖
And after this they stared inside the pot, and said that they saw
some shadows shaped like men. And she the denouncer declared
that she herself asked the two above mentioned [women] to cast
the lots. And she further declared that she retired to another
room during the time and act in which they cast, and that one
of those who was present told her that to the pot, and little reeds
they further added a scissor in a cross (...)

(...) they cast some lots which they said were the lots of
Saint Cyprian. And these were that, having a glass pot filled
with water, they took seven little reeds of the same size and
length as a finger, and they said these words; ‖ Blessed Saint
Cyprian, who seven lots in the sea thou cast, if good thou
cast them, better thou found them, by thy sanctity, and by my

virginity, show me what has happened to this man, if he is dead or alive ‖ And ending these words they cast one of the seven little reeds inside the pot, and they prayed one Creed, and this they repeated seven times. And in the end, they looked inside the pot, and she the denouncer did not see anything.

1683: Lisbon Inquisition, 57th Prosecutor's Notebook, fol.491v-492r.

Pt: (…) que lançasse agoa em hum vidro em forma de couilhente(?), por naõ ter ourinol nem dinheiro para o comprar onde melhor se podia fazer a ditta experiença segundo a ditta sua mestra disse, lançando ella confitente agoa no ditto vidro, e nove pedassinhos de juncos de huma esteira que a ditta sua mestra tirou, e ella confitente lançou na ditta agoa, dizendolhe que rezaçe nove credos sobre o mesmo vidro, e com effeito rezou, e fez benzer a mesma agoa com os dittos juncos, fazendo com cada hum sua cruz emquanto disia as palavras seguintes. | Bem aventurado S. Sypriano, as vossas sortes no mar ás lançantes, assim como bem ás lançastes melhor as apanhastes, pella vossa santidade, p[la] minha virgindade, que me mostreis aqui, se ha de Manoel da Costa de cazar com esta moça. E logo vio dentro na agoa que estava no ditto vidro hum moço, e huma moça, como se estivessem vivos com todas as feiçoes humanas de rosto e corpo (…) aquellas sortes ou experiençias se faziaõ melhor em ourinoẽs (…)

En: (…) that she cast water into a glass shaped as a (?), for not having a chamber pot, nor money to buy one, where this experiment would be better performed, according to what her mentioned master said, she the confessant casting water in the said glass, and nine little pieces of reed from a mat that her master took, and she the confessant cast in the said water, telling her to pray nine Creeds over the same glass, and indeed she prayed, and blessed the same water with the said reeds, making a cross with each one while saying the following words. | Blessed Saint Cyprian, thy lots in the sea thou cast, as thou cast them good, better thou picked them, by thy sanctity, by my virginity, show me here, if Manuel da Costa shall marry this girl. And immediately she saw in the water in the said glass a boy, and a girl, as if these were alive, with all the human features of their face and body (...) those lots or experiments were better performed in chamber pots (...)

1684: Lisbon Inquisition, 81ˢᵗ Prosecutor's Notebook, fol.315v, fol.321v-322r.

Pt: (...) tirou um vidro á feiçaõ de frasco, o qual encheo de agora da que ella denunciante tinha em hum pote, e cortando hum junco que tambem trazia, com huma thezoura, em nove partes, as lançou no ditto vidro, fazendo primeiro huã cruz com cada parte, havendo posto o ditto vidro sobre hum meyo alqueire, e este cuberto com hum lenço, rezou algumas oraçoẽs em vóz baixa, que ella denunciante naõ pode perceber, e depois o Padre Nosso em latim, de que ella denunciante sabe algumas pelavras, e dizendo a ella denunciante que visse o que se se mostrava na ditta agoa (...)

(...) enchendo de agoa qualquer vidro que fosse da boca larga, e dizendosse sobre elle as palavras seguintes, tomando primeiro nove palhinhas que se hiriaõ deitando dentro no ditto vidro, e dizendo a cada huma dellas, fazendo com a mesma o sinal da cruz: Bem aventurado Saõ Cipriaõ, fostes Bispo, e Arcebispo da caza de meu Senhor Jesus Christo, e nove sortes no már deitastes, bem as deitastes, melhor as apanhastes, pessovos pola vossa santidade, e pela minha virgindade (se for donzela) ou castidade (se o naõ for) que aqui me mostreis o que prettendo saber (declarando o que he) e logo rezar nove Padre Nossos e nove Ave Marias (…)

En: (…) she took out a glass shaped like a jar, which she filled with water that she the denouncer had in a pot, and cutting a reed, which she also carried, with a scissor, into nine pieces, cast them into the said glass, making first a cross with each piece, having placed the said glass over half an *alqueire*,[77] and this was covered with a tissue, she prayed some prayer in a low voice, which she the denouncer could not understand, and afterwards an Our Father in Latin, of which she the denouncer knows some words, and told her the denouncer to see what was being shown in the said water (…)

(…) filling any glass with a wide mouth with water, and saying over it the following words, firstly taking nine little straws which should be gradually cast into the mentioned glass, and saying these with each of them, making the same sign of the cross: Blessed Saint Cyprian, thou were a Bishop, and Archbishop of the house of my Lord Jesus Christ, and nine lots in the sea thou cast, good thou cast them, better thou took them, I ask thee by thy sanctity and by my virginity (if this is a damsel) or chastity (if this is not) that thou show me here what I intend to known (declaring what this is) and immediately pray nine Our Fathers and nine Hail Marys (…)

---

77 An old and variable Portuguese unit of measure for grain, equivalent to 13,1 liters in Lisbon. What is probably meant in this case is that the 'glass' was placed on top of a basket or bowl of half an *alqueire* of volume.

1704: Lisbon Inquisition, 80th Prosecutor's Notebook, fol.262v, fol.263r.

Pt: (…) vio q̃ tinhaõ as sobreditas hum prato com sal em sima de hum estrado onde dava sol e por sima do dito prato hum ourinol com agoa e lhe perguntaraõ as sobreditas se queria ella declarante ver seu marido, e respondendolhe q̃ estimaria m[to] vello, a dita Joanna Maria disse a oraçaõ seguinte – Bem aventurado Saõ Cipriano q̃ fostes Bispo e Arcebispo mestre da caza de meu Sr JESUS Christo as vossas nove sortes no mar as deitastes, se bem as deitastes melhor as apanhastes, p[la] vossa santidade com minha castidade, e a minha virgindade vos pesso q̃ me mostreis aqui nestas agoas claras a fulano (…)

(…) e quando se disseraõ as palavras p[la] minha castidade pos ella declarante a maõ sobre o orinol, e quando se repetiraõ, as palavras p[la] minha virgindade, pos a maõ sobre o mesmo orinol a dita Michaela pur ser donzela e acabada de dizer a ditta oraçaõ rezou a ditta Michaela hum Padre Nosso com huã Ave Maria e lançou huã palinha dentro do ditto orinol, a qual reza e ceremonia se fes por nove mezes na mesma forma e depois de q̃ offereceo a dita Michaela as ditas oraçoĕns dizendo ofereçovos Saõ Cipriaõ estas oraçoĕns p[a] q̃ mostre, nestas agoas claras a fulano se he morto ou vivo em qual parte q̃ esteja no mar ou na terra, e entaõ pos a ditta Michaela hum guardanapo sobre o dito orinol com hua thisoura em cruz e imediatamte vio ella confitente dentro do dito orinol ao dito seu marido clara e cristam[te] dentro em hum navio (…)

En: (…) she saw that the above mentioned [women] had a plate with salt on top of a platform where the Sun was shining, and over this plate a chamber pot with water, and the above mentioned asked her if she the declarant wanted to see her husband, and responding that she would greatly esteem to see him, the mentioned Joana Maria said the following prayer – Blessed Saint Cyprian who was a Bishop and Archbishop, master of the house of my Lord Jesus Christ, thy nine lots thou cast, better thou picked them, by thy sanctity, with my chastity, and my virginity, I ask thee that thou show me clearly in these waters this man (…)

(…) and when they said the words by my chastity she the declarant placed her hand over the chamber pot, and when the words by my virginity were repeated, the mentioned Micaela placed her hand over the same chamber pot, for being a damsel, and once the prayer was finished, the mentioned Micaela prayed an Our Father with a Hail Mary, and cast one straw inside the said chamber pot, which prayer and ceremony was done during nine months in the same way and then the mentioned Micaela offered the said prayer saying, I offer thee these prayers, Saint Cyprian, so as thou show, in these clear waters if this man is dead or alive, in whatever part of the sea or land he may be, and then the mentioned Micaela placed a napkin over the said chamber pot with a scissor in a cross and immediately she the confessant saw her husband inside the said chamber pot, clear and crystally, in a ship (…)

1729: Lisbon Inquisition, Trial nr. 7485, fol.76r-77r.

Pt: (…) hũ ourinol com augoa, dentro delle se lançou por cada huã vez hũ ovo dizendosse a oraçaõ seguinte: Bem aventurado Saõ Cipriano foste Bispo, e Arcebispo da caza de meu Sᵣ JESUS Christo em busca de vossa irmã andastes a qual achaste Santa, e Virgẽ como a buscareis, nove sortes deitaste, se bem as deitaste milhor as apanhaste, assim mostai nestas augoas turbas, e claras se vem, ou não fulano, q̃ era o marido da dita molher a qual oraçaõ ella confitente dizia quando deitava o ovo no dito ourinol, ou quando algumas das ditas molheres, q̃ estavaõ prezentes, o deitava, as quais ella confitente ensinava a dita oração, rezando hũ Padre nosso, e huã Ave Maria, offerecendo as ditas oraçoẽs ao dito Santo. E como de cada vez q̃ se deitava o dito ovo sahiaõ diferentes, se naõ pode assentar se era certo o vir o dᵒ homem ou naõ, e fazendo a sorte das cartas emquanto se embaralhavaõ dezia as palavras seguintes : Em nome da Santisima Trindade me descobrias aqui toda a verdade, e em Nome de Deos e de Christo crucificado, me desabras a verdade; e estendendosse as cartas em sinco carreiras pondosse o nome daquella pessoa q̃ hade vir em alguns dos Reys do baralho, ficando este na carreira do meio era certo a vir a dita pessoa a caza mas cahindo com efeito na dita carreira do meio o dito Rey com o nome do homem, naõ sahio certa (…)

En: (…) a chamber pot with water, inside this was cast each time an egg, while saying the following prayer: Blessed Saint Cyprian, thou were Bishop, and Archbishop of the house of my Lord Jesus Christ, in search of thy sister thou roamed, nine lots thou cast, if good thou cast them, better thou picked them, in this way show in these dark and clear waters, if this man is coming, who was the husband of the mentioned woman to whom she the confessant was saying the prayer while casting the egg in the said chamber pot, or when any of the women present cast it, to whom she the confessant taught the said prayer, praying an Our Father, and a Hail Mary, offering the said prayers to the mentioned Saint. And as each time the egg was cast these came out different, and one could not know if it was certain that that man would come or not, and making the lots of the cards, while shuffling, she said the following words: In the name of the Holiest Trinity discover for me here the whole truth, and in the name of God and the Crucified Christ, open the truth to me; and laying out the cards in five rows, and placing the name of that person who is to come in some of the Kings of the deck, if this was in the middle row it was certain that this person would come to the house, but indeed the said King with the man's name falling in the said middle row, this did not come out right (…)

1731: Lisbon Inquisition, Trial nr. 9809, fol.5r-5v.

Pt: (…) pedio hum orinol, e huma palha de esteira, hum pires com sal, e hum pano, ou rodilho para sobre ella assentar assentar o orinol, e agoa, q̃ deytou no ditto orinol; e cortando a palha com huma thesoira em nove pedaços os foy deytando hum a hum dentro no orinol, dizendo as palavras seguintes por nove vezes ao deytar cada pedaço de palha dentro no ditto orinol na forma seguinte: Bemaventurado Saõ Cepriam, Bispo, ou Arcebispo, confessor da Igreja de meu Senhor Jesus Christo as vossas nove sortes no mar deytastes, se bem as deytastes melhor apanhastes, peçovos pela vossa virtude e Santidade, mostreis nestas agoas, claras, e bellas se ha de cazar Maria com Manoel Rodrigues : e rezando hum Padre Nosso com huã Ave Maria, por nove vezes, a cada huma destas repetia por tres vezes fazendo huma cruz com a boca sobre a do orinol se tu tens pacto activo, ou passivo, de todo o renuncio, e offerencendo tudo ao Santo, poz huma thezoura em cruz sobre o orinol e o cobrio com hum pano e mandando buscar (?) (?) de candea de enfermar fez dous rolinho, e os poz acezo hum de huma parte e outro de outra (…)

En: (…) she asked for a chamber pot, and a straw from a mat, a saucer with salt, and a cloth, or rag to put the chamber pot on, and water, which she cast into the said chamber pot; and cutting the straw with a scissor into nine pieces was casting them one by one inside the chamber pot, saying the following words nine times while casting each piece of straw inside the said chamber pot in the following way: Blessed Saint Cyprian, Bishop, or Archbishop, confessor of the Church of my Lord Jesus Christ, thy nine lots in the sea thou cast, if good thou cast them, better thou picked them, I ask thee, by thy virtue and sanctity, show in these clear and beautiful waters if Maria is to be married with Manuel Rodrigues : and praying an Our Father with a Hail Mary, nine times, at each of these she repeated three times the making of a cross with her mouth over that of the chamber pot, if thou has an active or passive pact, of all I renounce, and offering everything to the Saint, she placed a scissor in a cross over the chamber pot and covered it with a cloth and had (?) (?) of a sick lamp brought and made two little rolls, and lit them in one side and the other (…)

1750: Lisbon Inquisition, Trial nr. 8877, fol.15v-16r.

Pt: (…) se quisesse saber alguma couza que estivesse para soceder, ou tivesse socedido em parte remota rezasse oraçaõ de Saõ Ciprianno, a qual lhe ensinou e era a seguinte: Bem avinturado Saõ Ciprianno Bispo, e Arcebispo, confessor da Santa caza de nosso Senhor Jesus Christo pellas vossas nove sortes, que no mar deitastes e na terra apanhastes, pela vossa santidade, e pela minha virgindade vos pesso me mostreis aqui fulla[no] (nomeando entaõ a pessoa de que queizesse ter noticia), e que dita esta oraçaõ tomasse hũ orinol cheyo de agua limpa, na qual havia lançar nove palhas, doas por cada ves, e as havia lansar em cruz, repetindo a sobredita oraçaõ, e logo pondo a boca sobre o orinol chamasse pela pessoa de quem queria saber, a qual se fosse viva lhe apareceria (…)

En: (…) should she want to know anything which was to happen, or had happened in a remote place, to pray the prayer of Saint Cyprian, which she taught and was the following: Blessed Saint Cyprian, Bishop, and Archbishop, confessor of the Holy house of our Lord Jesus Christ, by thy nine lots, which in the sea thou cast and on land thou took, by thy sanctity, and by my virginity, I ask thee to show me here this man (naming then the person of whom she wished to know), and that for the said prayer she took a chamber pot filled with clean water, in which she should cast nine straws, two at a time, and should cast them in a cross, repeating the above mentioned prayer, and immediately place her mouth over the pot and call the person of whom she wanted to know, who, should they be alive, would appear to them (…)

1750: Lisbon Inquisition, Trial nr. 1082, fol.40v-41r.

Pt: (…) e p^a isso lançou hũ ovo, e agua dentro em hũ ourinol, q̃ poz sobre hũ prato de sal na prez^a de hũa rapariga de 8 a. por ser n^{va}, como a delata afirmou, q̃ fosse virgem, e a esta deo nove palhas p^a hũa a hũa hir lançando, como lançou, dentro no ourinol cõ as palavras seg^{tes} q̃ lhe hia ensinado a delata : Bem aventurado Saõ Cypriano, fostes Bispo e Arceb^o, confessor da casa Sta de meu Sr Jesus Christo, sobre as ondas do mar andastes, as vossas 9 sortes no mar deitastes; se no mar as deitastes, na terra arrecadastes; p^{la} vossa santid^e e p^{la} m^a virgindade vos pesso que nestas aguas declareis se he morto, ou vivo An^{to} Roiz : e outras na forma seg^{te} : Bem aventurado S. Cypriano q̃ ao mundo subistes, e de ervas vos cobristes, tres bràdos destes p^{la} S^{ma} Trind^e, q̃ vos acodisse; e p^{lo} divino sustento, e p^{lo} divino sacram^{to} vos pesso q̃ me descobrais se he morto, ou vivo An^{to} Rioz : o q̃ tudo feito pòz a delata hũa tezoura em cruz na boca do dᵗᵒ ourinol, proferindo mais outras palavras em voz baixa, q̃ disse serem do Credo (...)

En: (...) and for this she cast an egg and water inside a chamber pot which she placed over a plate of salt in the presence of an eight year old girl who should be young, as the felon claimed, and a virgin, and to this she gave nine straws, for her to cast, one by one, as she did, into the chamber pot with the following words the felon taught her: Blessed Saint Cyprian, thou were a Bishop and Archbishop, confessor of the Holy house of my Lord Jesus Christ, over the waves of the sea thou roamed, thine nine lots in the sea thou cast; if in the sea thou cast them, on land thou kept them; by thy sanctity and by my virginity I ask that in these waters thou declare if António Rodriguez is dead or alive : and another in the following way : Blessed St. Cyprian who to the world thou rose, and of herbs thou covered thyself, three shouts thou gave for the Holiest Trinity to aid thee; and by the divine sustenance, and by the divine sacrament I ask thee to discover if António Rodriguez is dead or alive : which once all was done, the felon placed a scissor as a cross on the mouth of the said chamber pot, uttering some more words in a low voice, which she said were of the Creed (...)

Appendix 2B: Known Saint Cyprian
Hydromancy References with Absent or Incomplete Ritual Procedures

1607(?): National Library of Portugal, COD. 6353, fol.118v.

Pt: Snr S. Cipriano sorti deitastis no mar se boa a deitaste milhor a tirastis eu vos conjuro pella vossa santidade e polla minha Virgindado q̃ vos mi mostreis nista agoa limpa e clara tal e tal cousa e se não negra e escura.

En: Lord Saint Cyprian, lots thou cast in the sea, if good thou cast it, better thou took it, I summon thee by thy sanctity and by my virginity that thou show me in this clean and clear water this and that thing, and if not black and dark.

APPENDIX 2C: KNOWN SAINT CYPRIAN HYDROMANCY REFERENCES WITH ABSENT OR FRAGMENTED INCANTATIONS

1620: Lisbon Inquisition, 4th Prosecutor's Notebook, fol.362v-363v.

Pt: (...) e estando na ditta casa ambas sós e huã minina de pouca idade lhe disse a ditta dona Caterina que queria deitar huãs sortes pera ver se avia ella denunciante de casar e tendolhe dantes mandado comprar hum ourinol pera este feito lho mandou encher dagoa, e loguo lhe metteo duas palhas compridas de maneira que ficassem como ficaraõ em crux e posto o ourinol do chaõ que era dos chatos por baixo estando assentada iunto delle e hum rollo de cera incendido a ditta dona Caterina benseo o ditto ourinol fazendo lhe duas ou tres cruses com a maõ disendo huãs palavras baixo as quais ella testemunha não entendeo posto que lhas ouvio, e loguo lhe disse e ensinou a ella testemunha que bemsesse o ourinol duas ou tres veses como quando os cleriguos deitaõ bençaõ disendo iuntamente huas palavras que a ditta dona Caterina lhe hia ensinando, e dellas lhe lembram as seguintes | por minha virgindade e por vossa sanctidade que me mostreis aqui neste ourinol com quem hade casar, e feito isto estando sempre o rollo acezo disse a dona Caterina a ditta minina que olhassa se via dentro no ourinol hum homẽ e ella olhou e disse que o naõ via e loguo a ditta dona Caterina olhou disendo que bem sabia que naõ o via de ser por naõ ser donzella e ella testemunha tambem olhou e não vio entam homẽ e tomando o ourinol chegou a porta e torno a olhar ao sol (por lhe a dona Caterina lhe diser que tambem ao sol se olhava) e tendosse ia saido a dona Caterina pera fora, vio dentro no ourinol hum mancebo (...)

En: (…) and being both alone in the said house and a young girl, lady Caterina asked if she wanted to cast some lots to see if she the denouncer would marry, and having told her to buy a chamber pot beforehand for this purpose, told her to fill it with water, and immediately placed two long straws in a way that these were as a cross, and placing the chamber pot, which was one with a flat bottom, on the floor, and sitting near it, and a lit roll of wax, and the mentioned lady Caterina blessed the said chamber pot by doing two or three crosses with her hand, saying some words in a low voice, which she said the witness did not understand even if she heard them, and immediately she told and taught her the witness that she should bless the chamber pot two or three times, as when the priests cast blessings, saying some words with this that the mentioned lady Caterina was teaching her, and of these she remembers the following | by my virginity and by thy sanctity that thou show me here in this chamber pot with whom she shall marry, and having done this, being the roll always lit, lady Caterina told the said girl to look inside the chamber pot to see if she saw a man, and she looked and said she did not, and immediately the mentioned lady Caterina looked saying that she knew she could not see for not being a damsel, and she the witness also looked and did not see any man, and taking the chamber pot she got close to the door and looked once again under the Sun (for lady Caterina told her that one also looked under the Sun), and having Lady Caterina gone outside, she saw a boy inside the chamber pot (…)

1644: Lisbon Inquisition, 36th Prosecutor's Notebook, fol.4v.

Pt: Enchiaõ hũ orinol de agoa e deitavaõ duas palhinhas em nome daquelas duas pessoas q̃ se queriaõ bem e hũa estava obsente e era para ver (?) ahi se era vivo ou morto, e rezavaõ hũ padre nosso e huã Ave mᵃ e hũ credo e diziaõ huã oraçaõ de S. Cipriano q̃ ia se naõ lembraõ della e esperavaõ ver ahi se o obsente era vivo ou morto.

En: They filled a chamber pot with water and cast two straws inside, in the name of those two people who desired each other, and one was absent, and this was to see if they were alive or dead, and they prayed an Our Father, and a Hail Mary and a Creed, and they said the prayer of Saint Cyprian, which she no longer remembered, and they waited to see if the absent person was alive or dead.

1660: Lisbon Inquisition, 47th Prosecutor's Notebook, fol.310v-311r.

Pt: (…) lançou agoa em hum orinol e pós na boca do mesmo huã tizoura em crus e lançou na agoa huãs palhas de tanho naõ se lembra se foraõ nove se tres e entaõ disse estas palavras no tempo em q̃ lancou as palhas: Bem aventurado S. Cepriano pella vossa castidade (ou pella vossa santidade) e pella minha virgindade me mostray tal ou tal cousa. E que o dito ourinol estava naquelle tempo ao sol, e dittas as palavras disse a ditta Mᵑᵃ Marinha que fervia a agoa, mas ella denunciante a não vio ferver (…)

En: (…) she cast water in a chamber pot and placed over the mouth of this a scissor in a cross and cast into the water some mat straws, she does not remember if these were nine or three, and then she said these words, when she cast the straws: Blessed Saint Cyprian, by thy chastity (or by thy sanctity) and by my virginity, show me such and such thing. And that the said chamber pot was at that time under the Sun, and having said these words the mentioned Mariana Marinha said the water was boiling, but she the denouncer did not see it boil (…)

1662: Lisbon Inquisition, Trial nr. 7020, fol.18v, fol.20r-20v, fol.43v.

Pt: (…) se pos a fazer com ellas huã devoçaõ ou sortes de Saõ Cipriano, as quais se fazem com moças donzellas, e entrando ella em caza da ditta Mᵃ da Sylva na crescença(?) abria estando ao Sol, achou a sobreditta Maria da Sylva com as sobredittas donzelas com hum ourinol cheyo de agoa com hum guardanapo em mᵗᵃs dobras na boca e virado pa baixo com um palhas em crux dentro no ourinol, e ensinara as dittas moças q̃ fizessem certas cruzes sobre o ourinol de canto a canto, dizendo no mesmo tempo certas palavras (…)

(…) e tomou hum ourinol, e o encheo de agoa e lhe meteo huãs palhas em cruzes, q̃ eraõ nove e as deitou dentro na agoa q̃ estava no ourinol, e lhe pos na boca hum guardanapo em dobras, e huã thezoura em crux, e diziaõ huãs palavras pellos nove dias que Saõ Cipriano andou no mar, q̃ pella sua sanctidade, e pella sua castidade lhe mostrasse seu marido (…)

(…) tendo ella Re hum ourinol, e nelle agua e huãs palhas, disse a huãs moças donzellas que sobre elle fizessem certas cruzes de canto a canto, e que dissessem entre outras palavras as seguintes: Saõ Cypriano Bispo e Arcebispo, polo poder que

Deos vos deu, me mostrai meu marido. E dizendolhe as moças q̃ viaõ no ourinol huãs cordas, e huã pessoa por ellas entaõ explicou ella Re que aquillo significava que seu marido vinha pelo mar, e que se as palhas viesse para as bordas do ourinol era sinal que o ditto seu marido estava em terra.

En: (…) and she started doing a devotion or lots of Saint Cyprian with them, which are made with damsels, and she entering the house of Maria da Silva in the (?) (?) being under the Sun, she found Maria da Silva with the mentioned damsels with a chamber pot filled with water with a napkin with many folds over the mouth and turned down with some straws in a cross inside the chamber pot, and she taught the mentioned girls that they do certain crosses over the chamber pot, from corner to corner, saying, at the same time, certain words (…)

(…) and she took a chamber pot, and filled it with water, and placed inside this some straws in a cross, which were nine, and she cast these inside the water in the chamber pot, and placed over its mouth a folded napkin, and a scissor in a cross, and she said some words for the nine days that Saint Cyprian roamed the sea, that by his sanctity, and by her chastity he show her her husband (…)

(…) having her the defendant a chamber pot, and in it water and some straws, said to some damsel girls that they make certain crosses over it, from corner to corner, and say, among others, these words: Saint Cyprian, Bishop and Archbishop, by the power that God gave thee, show me my husband. And by the girls telling her that they saw some ropes in the chamber pot, and a person, she the defendant then explained that that meant her husband was coming by sea, and if the straws came to the sides of the chamber pot it was a sign that her husband was on land.

1699: Lisbon Inquisition, 70th Prosecutor's Notebook, fol.396v.

Pt: (…) tomando hum orinol cheio de agoa que pos em sima de hum prato que tinha sal e na boca do orinol huã tisoura em cruz tendo juntam[te] na caza huã candeia aceza e que a dita molher do salvador dissera as palavras seguintes estando o orinol na sobredita forma – Bem aventurado Saõ Siprianno Bispo, e Arcebispo confessor de meu Senhor Jesus Christo, as vossas nove sortes, que no mar deitates, se bem as deitastes melhor as apanhastes, e que esta cerimonia com as ditas palavras tornacem outra vez a fazer em sua caza e que as sobreditas palavras haveriaõ de ser ditas por huã rapariga ou mulher virgem (…) fizeraõ outra ves a dita cerimonia na forma que tem declarado acrecentando nella (?) Joanna Maria, molher dele denunciante, que era no dito tempo soltr[a] e de doze annos de idade que dicece as dittas palavras tendo na maõ nove palhinhas de junco que lançava no orinol todas as vezes que que repetia as ditas palavras (…)

En: (…) taking a chamber pot filled with water which she placed on top of a plate of salt, and over the mouth of the chamber pot a scissor in a cross having with this in the house a lit lamp, and the mentioned wife of Salvador said the following words the chamber pot being in the mentioned form – Blessed Saint Cyprian, Bishop and Archbishop, confessor of my Lord Jesus Christ, thy nine lots, which in the sea thou cast, if good thou cast them, better thou picked them, and that this ceremony with the said words should be done again in his home, and that the mentioned words should be said by a virgin girl or woman (…) they did the ceremony again in the declared form adding to it (?) Joana Maria, wife of him the denouncer, who at the said time was single and twelve years old, to say the mentioned words having in hand nine reed straws which she cast into the chamber pot every time she repeated the words (…)

1705: Lisbon Inquisition, 76th Prosecutor's Notebook, fol.18r.

Pt: (…) com hum orinol cheyo de agoa em sima de hum prato de sal e huma tizoira em cruz em sima e nove palhinhas de isteira dentro e o poz ao sol e me disse a mim por hella ser mall vista lhe visse o que via dentro eu lhe disse que via hum homem em huma cama mas eu naõ vi a ninguem a outro dia me disse hella se queria eu ver meu marido botasse outra sorte eu a botei com as palavras seguintes que me lembraõ que hella me imsinou bem aventurado Saõ Supriano bispo e arsebispo confesor da caza de meu senhor Jesus Christo aclaraime esta sorte que veyia eu nestas agoas claras a meu màrido mais palavras me emsinou hella, mas a mim me naõ lambraõ isto me fez dizer nove vezes e depois me perguntou que vira eu lhe disse que vira a meu marido porem naõ vi nada (…)

En: (…) with a chamber pot filled with water on a plate of salt and a scissor in a cross on top and nine mat straws inside, and she placed it under the sun, and told me, as she had bad sight, to look inside, and I told her I saw a man in a bed, but I did not see anyone, on the next day she told me that if I wanted to see my husband to cast another lot, and I did with the following words which I remember she taught me: Blessed Saint Cyprian, Bishop and Archbishop, confessor of the house of my Lord Jesus Christ, make clear to me this lot, that I may see my husband in these clear waters, and she taught more words, but I do not remember them, this she made me say nine times and afterwards asked me what I had seen, and I said I had seen my husband, but I, however, had seen nothing (…)

1731: Lisbon Inquisition, Trial nr. 4082, fol.97v.

Pt: (…) e lhe ensinara huma oraçaõ, q̃ chamava de Saõ Cypriano a qual faria na forma seguinte acendia duas vellas, e no meyo dellas punha hum orinol, quasi cheyo de agoa, e lhe deytou dentro nove palhinhas de esteira e disse certas palavras, q̃ a dita molher lhe ensinara e no dito ourinol vio huma Igreja de hum convento de frades (…)

En: (…) and taught her a prayer which she called of Saint Cyprian, which was done in the following way, she would light two candles, and in the middle of these place a chamber pot, near filled with water, and she cast nine straws from a mat and said certain words, that the mentioned woman taught her, and in the said chamber pot she saw the church of a friars' convent (…)

Appendix 2D: Known Saint Cyprian
Hydromancy References with Incomplete or Absent Ritual Procedures and Incantation

1620: Lisbon Inquisition, 2nd Prosecutor's Notebook, fol.475r.

Pt: (...) hum frade do Carmo que chama Fr. Fr^co Per^ra lhe ensinara hua devoçam do ourinol resando sobre elle a oraçam de S. Cidram polo mar e vindo huã pessoa innocente ve^a nelle o que querem ver (...)

En: (...) a Carmelite friar named Fr. Francisco Pereira taught her a devotion of the chamber pot, by praying over it the prayer of Saint Cyprian through the sea, and an innocent person can see in this what they want to see (...)

1623: Lisbon Inquisition, 1st Prosecutor's Notebook, fol.289r.

Pt: (...) e disse que bottassemos sortes pera sabermos de meu genro e ela, e eu e minha criada bottamos no orinol e as tirou minha criada, que he piquena, e donzela, e vimos a meu genro embarcar e desembarcar na India (...)

En: (...) and she told us to cast lots to learn of my son-in-law and she, and me and my servant cast these in the chamber pot, and these were taken by my servant, who is young, and a damsel, and we saw my son-in-law embarking and disembarking in India (...)

1625: Lisbon Inquisition, 7th Prosecutor's Notebook, fol.291v.

Pt: (…) ovio estar falando palavras e so percebeo perguntar ou ensinar a huã sua criada que dezia ser donzella de vinte annos por nome Maria (…) e a ensinava do que avia de fazer e dizia quando hade vir e tinha hai hum ourinol huãs palhas e huãs tantas candeinhas postas em carreira de sera delgadas como de rollo e huãs favas (…)

En: (…) she heard her saying words and she only understood that she was asking or teaching one of her servants, who she said was a damsel, and twenty years old, named Maria (…) and she was teaching her of what she should do and saying when she should come, and she had there a chamber pot, some straws and a few thin wax candles in a row and some favas (…)

1693: Lisbon Inquisition, 67th Prosecutor's Notebook, fol.41v.

Pt: (…) que logo lhe faria a devoçaõ de Saõ Cipriano p^a o que enchendo hum ourinol de agoa botandolhe dentro huãs palinhas disse sobre elle alguãs palavras de que não faz memoria, e entaõ chamando p^{la} ditta molher lhe dezia que olhasse porque dentro do ourinol estava seu marido, porem ella denunciante naõ vio nada dentro do ourinol, nem sabe que a ditta molher o visse.

En: (…) that she would do for her the devotion of Saint Cyprian, for which she filled a chamber pot with water, putting some straws inside this, and she said some words which she does not remember, and then, calling the mentioned woman, she told her to look, for her husband was in the chamber pot, however she the denouncer did not see anything inside the chamber pot, nor does she know if the mentioned woman saw him.

Appendix 2E: Castro Marim Saint Simeon
Hydromancy Reference

1696: Évora Inquisition, 38th Prosecutor's Notebook, fol.192r.

Pt: (…) e que thomara huã bacia com agoa, e no meio fizera huã crus cõ huã palha, e chamara huã moca, q̃ a sobreditta tinha em sua caza, por nome Maria, era donzela, a qual ia oie he defunta, e thomara huãs contas, e com ellas benzendo a agoa rezando sinco Padres Nossos, e sinco Ave Marias e huãs palavras ao Benaventurado Sam Simiam, as quais erão as seguintes, dizendo Bemaventurado S[to] Samiam fostes Bispo, e Arcebispo confessor de meu senhor Jusu Christo, as sortes no mar vos as deitastes se bem as deitastes, bem as colhestes p[a] vossa santidade, e a minha virgindade, q̃ me mostreis, aqui a Diogo Sobr[o], e a D[os] Lopes ff[os] da d[a] denunciante, e a seu genrro Luis da Silva, e a seu sobr[o] Manoel Jorge e outros camaradas, os quais estavaõ na cidade de Ceita por soldados, se sam mortos, ou vivos; e dittas as palavras sobredittas, disse a ditta Maria de defunta, vira as figuras das pesoas sobredittas; as quais estavaõ na ditta cidade de Ceita, bons, de saúde (…)

En: (…) and that she took a basin with water, and in the middle made a cross with a straw, and called a girl, who the abovementioned had in her home named Maria, who was a damsel, who is now dead, and she took some beads, and with them, blessing the water praying five Our Fathers, and five Hail Maries and some words to the Blessed Saint Simeon, which were the following, saying Blessed Saint Simion, thou were a Bishop and Archbishop, Confessor of my Lord Jesus Christ, the lots in the sea thou cast them, if well thou cast them, good thou picked them, by thy sanctity and my virginity, that thou shows me here, Diogo Sobreiro, and Domingos Lopes, sons of the mentioned denouncer, and her son-in-law, Luis da Silva, and her nephew Manuel Jorge and other comrades, who were in the city of Ceuta as soldiers, if these are dead or alive; and the mentioned words, the mentioned dead Maria said them, [and] saw the figures of the above mentioned people, who were in the mentioned city of Ceuta, well, in health (…)

APPENDIX 3: DEVOTIONS OF SAINT ERASMUS

1637: Lisbon Inquisition, Trial nr. 11579, fol.16r-16v, fol.70r-71r.

Pt: (...) a oraçaõ de Erasmo e era na forma seg^te. pos hum fugareyro novo acezo e huã figideira nova chea de azeite e dentro cinco trocidaz, e hum papel em que estava pintado hũ homẽ, com outros a modo de diabos, que lhe tiravaõ as tripas, o qual papel estava posto no chaõ e ao longo do papel tres vellas verdes acezas e a ditta donna Catherina andava descabellada passeando pella caza de canto a canto dizendo huãs palavras, das quais lhe naõ entendeo elle declarante, mais que chamar os diabos, e outras vezes dizer Erasmo, Erasmo, e tanto que a ditta Donna Catherina chegava a ver o azeite sahia huã grande lavareda p^a a ditta Donna Catherina, e isto per muitas vezes ate que se acabou o ditto azeite, e que antes de começar a oração disse a ditta Dona Catherina que se o d^o Manoel de Lima ouvesse de vir ficaria a frigideira sem se quebrar e que se naõ ouvesse de vir se havia de quebrar com hũ grande estalo.

(...) e q̃ fizesse pintar hum S Erasmo: a q̃ a d^a Comp^a fez: e entregou a ella R, que a pos no chaõ, e iunto della tres velas verdes acezas hum fugareiro acezo, e huã frigid^a nelle com meio quartilho de azeite, e nove torcidas postas em figura de hum sino samaõ: e disse tres vezes a oraçaõ seguinte: Erasmo, Erasmo, bispo, e perlado foste em a cidade de Neve(?) Patriarca foste; a filha del Rey Farao de si se namorou, e si della naõ, ella te quis a ti; e ti naõ a quiseste a ella; queixoza, e enoiada a seu Pay o contou, seo Pay queixoso, e enoiado, a prenderte mandou, nessa prizão tai grande Erasmo, Erasmo, Erasmo q̃ sentiste; senti vascas; e revascas, senti ancias, e reancias, senti ardores e fervores; porquem? Pella filha del Rey Farao, tantas

vascas, e revascas, e ardores, e fervores tenha; e nomeou certa
pessoa; que naõ possa aquietar, nem sucegar ate q̃ outra certa
pessoa que tambem nomeou, venha buscar Erasmo, Erasmo,
Erasmo aguilhons te puzeraõ, outros golpes te deraõ, malharaõ,
e remalharaõ; e nestes golpes Erasmo q̃ sentiste? Senti vascas,
e revascas, senti ancias, e reancias, senti ardores, e fervores.
porqẽ? Pella filha de el Rey Farao tantas vascas, e revascas; tantas
ancias, e reancias, tantos ardores, e fervores; tenha certa pessoa
que nomeou; por outra certa pessoa que tambem nomeou:
Erasmo, Erasmo, Erasmo os Iudeus ao campo te levaraõ, e
hum torno levaraõ, a barriga te abriraõ, as tripas te fiaraõ; neste
taõ g^{de} tromento Erasmo q̃ sentiste? Senti vascas, e revascas,
senti ardores, e fervores, ancias e reancias; porquem? Pella
filha del Rey Farao; tantas ancias, e reancias, tantos ardores, e
fervores, tantas vascas e revascas, tenha certa pessoa q̃ nomeou
por outra certa pessoa que tambem nomeou; que naõ possa
aquietar Erasmo, Erasmo, Erasmo q̃ neste taõ grande torm^{to}
desesperaste, e ao inferno te foste por q̃ la estas eu te conjuro com
Barsabu, eu coniuro com q^{tos} demonios no inferno estaõ; todos
iuntos vos ajunteis; aonde estiver certa pessoa q̃ nomeou ahy vos
ireis; em seo corpo vos aposentareis, q̃ não possa aquietar, nem
socegar ate q̃ logo venha buscar a certa pessoa que tambem
nomeou; Erasmo, Erasmo eu te coniuro com quantos demonios
ha no matadiro; com q^{tos} demonios os ha na carnuaria; com
q^{tos} demonios ha na pescadaria; com quantos demonios ha no
rastro; eu te coniuro com quantos demonios ha no rio; com q^{tos}
demonios os ha em becos, e em cantinhos do mundo, de mar a
mar compatim compatim com Barrabazão com Mª de Padilha,
com toda sua quadrilha todos iuntos vos ajuntas aonde estiver
certa pessoa q̃ nomeou ireis em seo corpo vos recolhereis q̃ naõ
possa aquietar, nem sucegar, nem com nenhuã m^{er} gosto tomar;
ate que com certa pessoa q̃ nomeou venha dar: Erasmo, Erasmo
eu te conjuro com o Pay que te fez, com a May que te pario,

com a part^a que te partiu, com as vestiduras que te puzeraõ com as ordens, que te deraõ, com a vida que viveste; com a morte que morreste, com a desesperaçaõ q̃ desesperaste, que tantas vascas, e revascas tenha certa pessoa que nomeou; e dizendo a ditta oração tomava ella R o cospo da boca, e o deitava na frigideira, e com hum capato na maõ açoutava o d^{to} S Erasmo dandolhe tres açoutes coniurando primeiro todos os demonios do inferno, e o dinr^o com q̃ se compravaõ as d^{as} couzas q̃ sempre se compravaõ de novo cada vez q̃ ella R fazia a d^a oraçaõ a qual fez por nove vezes; e ajuntou dores e esconjuros de demonios horrendos e temerosos com os quais sahiaõ da d^a fregid^a huãs lavaredas p^a ella R mostrando a hiaõ buscar; ao que ella R respondia: não a my; não a my; la; la aonde esta certa pessoa q̃ então nomeava (…)

En: (…) the prayer to Saint Erasmus and it was in the following way, she set a new lit stove and a new frying pan filled with olive oil and inside five wicks, and a paper where there was a man painted, with others looking like devils, who were taking out his guts, which paper was on the floor, and along this paper three green lit candles and the mentioned Lady Catherina was uncombed walking through the room, from corner to corner, saying some words, which he the declarer did not understand, but that these called on devils, and other times said 'Erasmus, Erasmus', and when the mentioned Lady Catherina came to see the olive oil, great flames would come out towards the mentioned Lady Catherina, and this for many times until the said olive oil ran out, and that before the prayer started the mentioned Lady Catherina said that if the mentioned Manuel Lima was to come the frying pan would remain without breaking, and if he did not come it would break with a great noise.

(…) and that she had a Saint Erasmus painted; which the said companion did, and gave it to her the defendant, who placed this on the floor, and near it three lit green candles, a lit stove, and a frying pan on it with a quarter *quartilho*[78] of olive oil, and nine wicks placed in the shape of a pentagram; and she said the following prayer three times: Erasmus, Erasmus, bishop, and prelate, in the city of Neneveh(?) Patriarch thou were; the daughter of King Pharao in love with thee she fell, and thee not with her, she wanted thee, and thou did not want her; complaining and bothered to her Father she told, her Father complaining and bothered, thy arrest he ordered, in that great prison Erasmus, Erasmus, Erasmus, what did thou feel? I felt lashes, and relashes; I felt urges, and reurges; I felt burnings and fervors; for whom? For the daughter of King Pharao, so many lashes, and relashes, burnings, and fervors may have; and she named a certain person; may they not be able to stop, nor rest, until another certain person she also named, they come to take, Erasmus, Erasmus, Erasmus, shackles they placed on thee, other blows they gave thee, they mauled, and remauled thee; and in these blows Erasmus, what did thou feel? I felt lashes, and relashes, I felt urges, and reurges, I felt burnings, and fervors. For whom? For the daughter of King Pharao, so many lashes, and relashes; so many urges, and reurges, so many burnings and fervors; may a certain person she named have; for another person she also named; Erasmus, Erasmus, Erasmus, the Jews to the field took thee, and a lathe they took, thy belly they opened, thy guts they spindled; in this such great torment, Erasmus, what did thou feel? I felt lashes, and relashes, I felt burnings and fervors, urges, and reurges; for whom? For the daughter of King Pharao; so many urges, and reurges, so many burnings, and fervors, so many lashes, and relashes; may a certain person she named have for another person she also named; may they not

---

78 An old Portuguese unit of measurement for liquids equivalent to 0,35 liters.

stop Erasmus, Erasmus, Erasmus who in this such great torment thou despaired, and to hell thou went, and there thou are, I conjure thee with Barsabu, I conjure thee with as many demons as are in hell; all gather; where a certain person she named is, there thou shall go, in their body take residence, may they not stop, nor rest until they come to take a certain person she also named; Erasmus, Erasmus I conjure thee with as many demons as are in the slaughterhouse; with as many demons as are in the meat market; with as many demons as are in the fishery; with as many demons as are in the rake; I conjure thee with as many demons as are in the river; with as many demons as are in the alleys, and corners of the world, from sea to sea come(?) come(?) with Barrabazão, with Maria de Padilha, with all her gang, all gather wherever is a certain person she named, go into their body, that they may not stop, nor rest, nor take pleasure with any woman, until they come to a certain person she named; Erasmus, Erasmus, I conjure thee with the Father who made thee, with the Mother who birthed thee, with the midwife who brought thee, with the vestments they placed on thee, with the orders they gave thee, with the life thou lived, with the death thou died, with the desperation thou despaired, that so many lashes, and relashes may a certain person she named take; and saying the mentioned prayer she the defendant took spit from her mouth, and cast it into the frying pan, and with a shoe in her hand she would hit the mentioned Saint Erasmus, giving it three blows, first conjuring all the demons in hell, and the money with which all the new things she the defendant used in the said prayer where bought with, which was done nine times; and she added pains and horrible and fearful summonings of demons, with which flames would come out of the frying pan towards her the defendant, as if wanting to get her; to which she the defendant responded: not to me; not to me; there, there, where a certain person she named was (...)

1645: Lisbon Inquisition, Trial nr. 7536, fol.76r-76v.

Pt: Ó Benaventurado santo erasmo, santo Bispo, e Arcebispo, Papa, Cardeal, na casa santa de Roma de meo Senhor Jesu Christo. El Rey Pia vos mandou chamar, ao monte olivete vos mandou levar, as vossas tripas vos mandou tirar, em hũ parafuso volas mandou parafusar, em hũ sarilho sarilhou, em huã dobadoura dobar, no golfo do mar volas mandou botar, com a vossa santidade as fostes tirar, em huã frigideira d'azeite volas cozeraõ, em huã casa escura volas metteraõ. Por aquelles ardores, e fervores que tivestes que vôs vos lenvanteis, e vos encorporeis, e no coraçaõ de fulano entreis, e o inquieteis, ou aquieteis (conforme ao que se pretendias, mas sempre pera violentar a vontade da pessoa) e que pera este efeito tinha huã pintura do ditto Santo (…)

En: Oh Blessed Saint Erasmus, holy Bishop, and Archbishop, Pope, Cardinal, in the holy house of Rome of my Lord Jesus Christ. King Pia had thou called, to Mount Olivetti he had thou brought, thy guts he ordered to be taken, in a screw he had them screwed, in a reel, reeled, in a folder, folded, in the gulf of the sea he had them dropped, with thy sanctity thou took them, in a frying pan of olive oil they boiled them, in a dark house they placed them. By those burnings, and fervors thou had, rise, and incorporate, and in the heart of this person enter, and disquiet them, or quiet them (according to what is desired, but always to violate a person's will), and for this effect she had a painting of the mentioned Saint Erasmus made (…)

1662: Lisbon Inquisition, Trial nr. 7020, fol.17v, fol.19r.

Pt: (…) e loguo armou huã meza pondo nella huãs vellas de cera verde, hum copo de vinho, dous prattos emborcados, hum em sima do outro com real e m° dentro, e hum pequeno de queijo e hum paõ de (?) e huã faca, e hum papel com S^to Erasmo pintado, e ella ditta Maria da Sylva se despio em camiza, e atandoa pella cintura, deixava cair dos hombros a camiza, e ficava nua da cintura p^a sima, e com os cabellos estendidos abaixo, e passeando pella caza de canto a canto, dizia as palavras seguintes.

Bem aventurado S Erasmo Bispo e Arcebispo confessor da caza de meu snor Jesu Christo; El Rey Herodes vos mandou chamar p^a vos manifestar se quirieis ser da sua ley; vos lhe dissestes q̃ naõ, que queireis ser da ley de meu senhor Jesu xpo; elle vos mandou chamar, e em hum banco de ferro vos mandou amarrar, com varas de ferro cruelm^te vos mandou açoutar, as vossas tripas pelo vosso embigo vos mandou tirar, em hum sarilho as mandou sarilhar, em hum parafuso as mandou parafusar; em talhas de azeite volas mandou aferventar, pello mar abaixo volas mandou deitar, por aquelles ardores, e fervores que tivestes, elles mesmo dai no coraçaõ de fulano (nomeando o seu esposo) que naõ possa dormir, nem comer, nem socegar, atee me naõ vir buscar (…)

(…) e foi que armara huã meza, e punha nellas tres candeinhas de cera verde q̃ punha nos cantos da meza punha hum papel em q̃ estava pintada huã figura e homem, q̃ dizia q̃ era s^to Erasmo que tinha no embigo hum buraquinho, e por elle hũ cordel pello qual puxava q̃ dezia a Oraçaõ abaixo escrita e hia emburilhando em hum novello, e punha mais dous prattos hum em sima do outro com hũ real e m°, e hum merendr°, e hum pequeno de queijo, e hum copo de vinho, e tudo ao outro dia se dava ao pr° pobre q̃ vinha á porta e a oraçaõ, e palavras q̃ dizia eraõ as seg^tes. S^to Erasmo Bispo e Arcebispo

confessor da caza de meu senhor Jesu Xpo El Rey Herodes
vos mandou chamar pᵃ vos manifestar se quirieis ser da sua ley
vos lhe dissestes q̃ naõ, q̃ querieis ser da ley do meu Senhor
Jesus Xpo; elle vos mandou tomar, e a hum banco de ferro vos
mandou deitar e amarrar, as vossas sagradas tripas, pello vosso
sagrado embigo volas mandou tirar, e volas mandou ennovellar,
em tinas de azeite volas mandou enferventar, pello mar abaixo
volas mandou deitar, por aquelles ardores, e fervores, e amores
q̃ tivestes, elle mesmos dey no coraçaõ de fulano, q̃ era a pessoa
que precuravaõ, q̃ naõ pudesse estar, nem sossegar, nem dormir
atee(?) com a pessoa naõ vir fallar, e outras palavras e q̃ ella se
não lembra; o q̃ fazia de noite a dez horas (…)

En: (…) and immediately set a table placing on it some green
wax candles, a glass of wine, two plates upside down, one on
top of the other with a *real* and a half [coin] inside, and a
piece of cheese and a (?) bread, and a knife, and a paper with a
painting of Saint Erasmus, and her, Maria da Silva, undressed
to her shirt, and tying it by the waist, let the shirt fall from her
shoulders, and was naked from the waist up, and with her hair
down, and walking through the room, from corner to corner,
said the following words. Blessed Saint Erasmus, Bishop and
Archbishop, confessor of the house of my Lord Jesus Christ;
King Herod had thou called to manifest if thou wanted to be
of his law; thou told him no, that thou wanted to be of the law
of my Lord Jesus Christ; he had thou called, and in an iron
bench had thou tied, with iron rods cruelly had thou beat, thy
guts through thy bellybutton had them pulled, in a reel he had
them reeled, in a screw he had them screwed; in pot of olive oil
he had them boiled, down the sea he had them cast, by those
burnings, and fervors thou had, these same give into the heart
of this person (naming her husband) that he may not sleep, nor
eat, nor rest, until he does not come to get me (…)

(...) and it was that she set a table, and placed on it three candles of green wax, which she placed on the corners of the table, placed a paper in which the figure of a man was painted, who she said was Saint Erasmus, who had a small hole in his bellybutton, and a cord coming through it, which was being pulled, and said the prayer written below, while wrapping a ball of thread, and she placed two more plates, one on top of the other with a *real* and a half, and a piece of bread, a piece of cheese, and a glass of wine, and everything was to be given the next day to the first beggar who knocked on the door, and the prayer and words she said were the following: Saint Erasmus, Bishop and Archbishop, confessor of the house of my Lord Jesus Christ. King Herod had thou called to manifest if thou wanted to be of his law, thou told him no, that thou wanted to be of the law of my Lord Jesus Christ; he had thou taken, and to an iron bench had thou laid and tied, thy holy guts, through thy sacred bellybutton he had them taken, and had them wrapped, in bowls of olive oil he had them boiled, down the sea he had them cast, by those burnings, and fervors, and loves which thou had, these give onto the heart of this person, who was the person she was seeking, may they not be, nor rest, nor sleep, until with this person they do not come to speak, and other words she did not remember; and this she did at night, at ten o'clock (...)

1663: Lisbon Inquisition, Trial nr. 10487, fol.11r-11v.

Pt: (...) a ditta helena fig[ra] emprestou à d[ta] D. Innes por via della confitente a figura de Santo Erasmo dibuxada em hum purgaminho no qual estava lançado o santo, e os fariseus tirandolhe as tripas, e que ella confitente para que a ditta dona Ines podesse usar do Santo Erasmo para conseguir o seu intente lhe ensinou o modo e a reza que se lhe havia de fazer pondolhe tudo em hum papel no qual se continha que havia de por o santo em hum oratorio e posta de juelhos deante delle com huã candeia aceza havia de dizer a oraçaõ seguinte: Bem aventurado Santo Erasmo santo bem aventurado, o perdido e o ganhado foste Bispo e Arcebispo, e Cardeal e Papa em Roma, e confessor de meu Senhor Jesu Christo, elle vos mandou atar rigorosamente em hum banco de ferro, e tirar vossas tripas pello embigo com parafuso de ferro, num sarilho de ferro volas ensarilharam, numa dobadoura de ferro volas dobaram, numa caldeira de azeite e breu volas a ferventaram, no mar sagrado volas deitarao, peçovos bem aventurado santo por aquelles ardores e fervores que sentistes em vosso coraçaõ quando las tiraram essas deis a fulano para que me faça o que lhe peço : e que esta oração se fazia treze dias trez vezes cada dia rezando de cada ves treze padre nossos treze Ave Marias treze Credos, e acrescentando cada dia huã candea de modo que no ultimo dos treze viessem a ser outras tantas as candeas e que não sabe ella confitente se a dita Dona Ines usou desta oração (...)

En: (...) the mentioned Helena Figueira lent to the mentioned Lady Inês through her the confessant the figure of Saint Erasmus, drawn on a scroll, in which the saint was laying down, and the Pharisees removing his guts, and that she the confessant, so as the mentioned Lady Ines could make use of Saint Erasmus to achieve her intent, taught her the way and prayer which should be done to him, placing everything on a piece of paper in which was contained that one should place the saint in an oratory and on one's knees in front of him, with a lit candle/lamp, should say the following prayer: Blessed Saint Erasmus, blessed saint, the lost and the found, thou were Bishop and Archbishop, and Cardinal and Pope in Rome, and confessor of my Lord Jesus Christ, he had thou rigorously tied to an iron bench, and thy guts taken from thy bellybutton with an iron screw, in a reel they reeled them, in an iron folder, they folded them, in a pot of olive oil and pitch they boiled them, in the sacred sea they cast them, I ask thee, blessed saint, by those burnings and fervors, which thou felt in thy heart when they took them out, give those to this person so as they will do what I ask; and this prayer was done thirteen days in a row, three times per day, praying each time thirteen Our Fathers, thirteen Hail Marys, thirteen Creeds, and adding on each day one candle/lamp, in such a way that on the last day of the thirteen this would be the number of candles/lamps, and she the confessant does not know if the mentioned Lady Ines used this prayer (...)

Martyrdom of Saint Erasmus. Engraving by G.M. Mitelli after N. Poussin.

Appendix 4A: Alternative fava baptism

1645: Lisbon Inquisition, Trial nr. 7536, fol.46r-46v.

Pt: (…) indo no mez de Agosto passado, segundo sua lembrança a igreja da See desta cidade e tendo na maõ esquerda as dittas favas, tomou com a maõ direita agua benta da pia, e botou alli na testa e tambem as favas dizendolhe eu vos baptizo, em nome do Pᵉ, e do filho e do Spirito Santo, e depois destarem baptizadas, lhes disse, eu vos esconjuro naõ por favas senaõ por homẽ e molheres, com Saõ Pedro e Saõ Paulo e com o Apostolo Santiago que vos mee declareis esta verdade, com o portal de Betlem, e dos Santos q̃ morreraõ em Jerusalem, e com a Sᵐᵃ Trindade, assy como Ds abrio as carreyras aos filhos de Israel, assy abraes caminho e carreyra, e me mostreis o que vos pesso (…)

En: (…) going in the past month of August, according to her memory, to the cathedral of this city and having the said favas in her left hand, she took holy water from the basin with her right hand, and put this there on her forehead and also the favas, saying to them, I baptize thee, in the name of the Father, and the Son, and the Holy Spirit, and after they were baptized she said to them, I conjure thee, not as favas, but as men and women, with Saint Peter and Saint Paul and with the Apostle Saint James, that thou declare to me this truth, with the gate of Bethlehem, and the Saints who died in Jerusalem, and with the Holiest Trinity, as God opened the roads to the children of Israel, so may thou open the path and road, and show me what I ask (…)

Appendix 4B: Alternative fava casting incantation

1637: Lisbon Inquisition, Trial nr. 11579, fol.64v.

Pt: (…) favas tomo, naõ tomo favas e tomo o coraçaõ de tal pessoa que ahy nomeou, favas tomo naõ tomo favas tomo o coraçaõ de tal pessoa cujo nome ahy declarou, e esconjurando as ditas favas em nome da Santissima Trindade e da Virgem Snra Nossa, pera que dissessem a verdade (…)

En: (…) favas I take, favas I do not take, but I take the heart of this person who she named, favas I take, favas I do not take, I take the heart of this person she named, and conjuring the said favas in the name of the Holiest Trinity and the Virgin Our Lady, so as they would tell the truth (…)

1672: Lisbon Inquisition, Trial nr. 12722, fol.4r.

Pt: (…) eu te esconjuro favas naõ como favas, senão como creaturas, com nove homens, e nove molheres, com as tres pessoas da Santissima Trind^e com tres Clerigos revestidos no altar com as tres Missas da noite de Natal, com os tres Livros missaes, com o mar, e com as sacras, com os ventos, e com todos os elementos |, e fazendo entaõ tres cruses sobre o chaõ lançava as dittas favas das maõs nelle dizendo-lhes | minhas mininas, minhas queridas, minhas amadas, declaraime aqui esta verdade assim com Deos apartou a noite do dia, assim me declarai vos a verdade nestas cinco sortes (…)

En: (…) I conjure thee favas, not as favas, but as creatures, as nine men, and nine women, with the three persons of the Holiest Trinity, with three invested priests at the altar, with the three masses of Christmas, with the three Missal books, with the sea, and with the sacred, with the winds, and with all the elements |, and then making three crosses over the floor she cast the favas from her hands onto it saying | my girls, my dears, my beloved, declare to me here this truth, as God separated the night from the day, thus may thou declare the truth in these five lots (…)

BIBLIOGRAPHY

MANUSCRIPT

Arquivo Nacional da Torre do Tombo (ANTT):
Tribunal do Santo Ofício 1536/1821. Inquisição de Coimbra, Processos, nr. 5634, *Processo de Pedro Afonso*, 1621.

Tribunal do Santo Ofício 1536/1821. Inquisição de Coimbra 1541/1821, Promotor, *124º Caderno do Promotor: 2.ª Série*, 1784-1802.

Tribunal do Santo Ofício 1536/1821. Inquisição de Évora 1536/1821, Promotor, *38º Caderno do Promotor*, 1659-1698.

Tribunal do Santo Ofício 1536/1821. Inquisição de Lisboa 1536/1821, Cadernos do Promotor, *1º Caderno do Promotor*, 1610-1624.

Tribunal do Santo Ofício 1536/1821. Inquisição de Lisboa 1536/1821, Cadernos do Promotor, *2º Caderno do Promotor*, 1606-1624.

Tribunal do Santo Ofício 1536/1821. Inquisição de Lisboa 1536/1821, Cadernos do Promotor, *3º Caderno do Promotor*, 1596-1625.

Tribunal do Santo Ofício 1536/1821. Inquisição de Lisboa 1536/1821, Cadernos do Promotor, *4º Caderno do Promotor*, 1606-1624.

Tribunal do Santo Ofício 1536/1821. Inquisição de Lisboa 1536/1821, Cadernos do Promotor, *7º Caderno do Promotor*, 1607-1625.

Tribunal do Santo Ofício 1536/1821. Inquisição de Lisboa 1536/1821, Cadernos do Promotor, *17º Caderno do Promotor*, 1631-1639.

Tribunal do Santo Ofício 1536/1821. Inquisição de Lisboa 1536/1821, Cadernos do Promotor, *19º Caderno do Promotor*, 1634-1642.

Tribunal do Santo Ofício 1536/1821. Inquisição de Lisboa 1536/1821, Cadernos do Promotor, *30° Caderno do Promotor*, 1642-1649.

Tribunal do Santo Ofício 1536/1821. Inquisição de Lisboa 1536/1821, Cadernos do Promotor, *36° Caderno do Promotor*, 1644-1659.

Tribunal do Santo Ofício 1536/1821. Inquisição de Lisboa 1536/1821, Cadernos do Promotor, *37° Caderno do Promotor*, 1651-1660.

Tribunal do Santo Ofício 1536/1821. Inquisição de Lisboa 1536/1821, Cadernos do Promotor, *47° Caderno do Promotor*, 1656-1670.

Tribunal do Santo Ofício 1536/1821. Inquisição de Lisboa 1536/1821, Cadernos do Promotor, *50° Caderno do Promotor*, 1670-1674.

Tribunal do Santo Ofício 1536/1821. Inquisição de Lisboa 1536/1821, Cadernos do Promotor, *57° Caderno do Promotor*, 1659-1684.

Tribunal do Santo Ofício 1536/1821. Inquisição de Lisboa 1536/1821, Cadernos do Promotor, *67° Caderno do Promotor*, 1684-1694.

Tribunal do Santo Ofício 1536/1821. Inquisição de Lisboa 1536/1821, Cadernos do Promotor, *70° Caderno do Promotor*, 1688; 1694-1699.

Tribunal do Santo Ofício 1536/1821. Inquisição de Lisboa 1536/1821, Cadernos do Promotor, *75° Caderno do Promotor*, 1696-1711.

Tribunal do Santo Ofício 1536/1821. Inquisição de Lisboa 1536/1821, Cadernos do Promotor, *76° Caderno do Promotor*, 1690-1710.

Tribunal do Santo Ofício 1536/1821. Inquisição de Lisboa 1536/1821, Cadernos do Promotor, *80° Caderno do Promotor*, 1699-1714.

Tribunal do Santo Ofício 1536/1821. Inquisição de Lisboa 1536/1821, Cadernos do Promotor, *81° Caderno do Promotor*, 1677-1710.

Tribunal do Santo Ofício 1536/1821. Inquisição de Lisboa 1583/1821, Processos, nr. 247, *Processo de Antónia da Serra*, 1672-1673.

Tribunal do Santo Ofício 1536/1821. Inquisição de Lisboa 1583/1821, Processos, nr. 1082, *Processo de Joanna Rosa*, 1750.

Tribunal do Santo Ofício 1536/1821. Inquisição de Lisboa 1583/1821, Processos, nr. 1550, *Processo de Francisco*, 1743.

Tribunal do Santo Ofício 1536/1821. Inquisição de Lisboa 1583/1821, Processos, nr. 4082, *Processo de D. Paula Teresa de Miranda Souto-Maior*, 1731-1735.

Tribunal do Santo Ofício 1536/1821. Inquisição de Lisboa 1583/1821, Processos, nr. 5723, *Processo de Paula de Moura*, 1673-1674.

Tribunal do Santo Ofício 1536/1821. Inquisição de Lisboa 1583/1821, Processos, nr. 7020, *Processo de Maria da Silva*, 1662-1664.

Tribunal do Santo Ofício 1536/1821. Inquisição de Lisboa 1583/1821, Processos, nr. 7485, *Processo de Domingas Maria*, 1729.

Tribunal do Santo Ofício 1536/1821. Inquisição de Lisboa 1583/1821, Processos, nr. 7536, *Processo de Marta Nogueira*, 1645.

Tribunal do Santo Ofício 1536/1821. Inquisição de Lisboa 1583/1821, Processos, nr. 8465, *Processo de Jerónima de Almeida*, 1690.

Tribunal do Santo Ofício 1536/1821. Inquisição de Lisboa 1583/1821, Processos, nr. 8877, *Processo de Teresa Maria*, 1751-1761.

Tribunal do Santo Ofício 1536/1821. Inquisição de Lisboa

1583/1821, Processos, nr. 9667, *Processo de Maria da Cunha*, 1648-1649.

Tribunal do Santo Ofício 1536/1821. Inquisição de Lisboa 1583/1821, Processos, nr. 9809, *Processo de D. Maria Antónia*, 1731.

Tribunal do Santo Ofício 1536/1821. Inquisição de Lisboa 1583/1821, Processos, nr. 10067, *Processo de Maria Rosa de Jesus*, 1731.

Tribunal do Santo Ofício 1536/1821. Inquisição de Lisboa 1583/1821, Processos, nr. 10487, *Processo de Constantina da Távora*, 1663-1664.

Tribunal do Santo Ofício 1536/1821. Inquisição de Lisboa 1583/1821, Processos, nr. 11579, *Processo de D. Catarina Ribeira*, 1637-1639.

Tribunal do Santo Ofício 1536/1821. Inquisição de Lisboa 1583/1821, Processos, nr. 12722, *Processo de Catarina de Sousa*, 1672.

Biblioteca Nacional de Portugal (BNP):
Delgado, João, *Astrologia Pratica*, COD. 6353, 1607.

PRINTED

Ali, ConjureMan, *Saint Cyprian: Saint of Necromancers*, West Yorkshire: Hadean Press, 2011.

Anon., *O Grande Livro de S. Cypriano: ou Thesouro do Feiticeiro*, Lisbon: Livraria Economica, n.d.

Azzi, Riolando, 'O Casamento na Sociedade Colonial Luso-Brasileira: Uma Análise Histórico-Teológica', *Perspectiva Teológica* 24 (1992): 49-66.

Barthold, Erzebet, *Cyprianic Cartomancy*, West Yorkshire: Hadean Press, 2016.

Basset, René, *Les Apocryphes Éthiopiens – IV: Les Prières de S. Cyprien et de Théophile*, Milan: Archè, 1982.

Bethencourt, Francisco, *O Imaginário da Magia: Feiticeiras, Adivinhos e Curandeiros em Portugal no Século XV*, São Paulo: Companhia das Letras, 2004.

Björn Gårdbäck, Johannes, 'Cyprianus Förmaning', in Cummins, Alexander, Hathaway Diaz, Jesse and Zahrt, Jennifer (eds.), *Cypriana: Old World*, Seattle: Revelore Press, 2017: 36–50.

Castello Branco, Camillo, *A Filha do Arcediago*, Porto: Casa de Cruz Coutinho – Editor, 1868.

Castro Vicente, Félix Francisco, 'O Libro de San Cibrán: Unha Realidade no Imaxinario Popular', *Murguía: Revista Galega de Historia* 12 (2007): 69–104.

Duni, Matteo, 'Esorcisti o Stregoni? Identità Professionale del Clero e Inquisizione a Modena nel Primo Cinquecento', *Mélanges de l'Ecole Française de Rome, Italie et Méditerranée*, 115:1 (2003): 263–85.

Leitão, José, *Opuscula Cypriani: Variations on the Book of Saint Cyprian and Related Literature*, West Yorkshire: Hadean Press, 2019.

Leitão, José, 'Searching for Cyprian: in Portuguese Ethnography', in Cummins, Alexander, Hathaway Diaz, Jesse and Zahrt, Jennifer (eds.), *Cypriana: Old World*, Seattle: Revelore Press, 2017: 117-162.

Leitão, José, *The Book of St. Cyprian: The Sorcerer's Treasure*, West Yorkshire: Hadean Press, 2014.

Leitão, José Vieira, 'Seeking Voices and Finding Meaning: An Analysis of Portuguese Verbal Divination', *Incantatio* 6 (2017): 155-169.

Londoño, Marcela, *Las Oraciones Censuradas: Superstición y Devoción en los Índices de Libros Prohibidos de España y Portugal (1551-1583)*, Barcelona: Herder Editorial, 2019.

Paiva, José Pedro, *Bruxaria e Superstição num País Sem "Caça às*

Bruxas" 1600–1774, Lisbon: Editorial Notícias, 2002.

Souza, Laura de Mello, *The Devil and the Land of the Holy Cross: Witchcraft, Slavery and Popular Religion in Colonial Brazil*, Austin: University of Texas Press, 2003.

Stratton-Kent, Jake, 'Seven Years the Sea Thou Roamed: Cyprianic Ritual and Divination', in Cummins, Alexander, Hathaway Diaz, Jesse and Zahrt, Jennifer (eds.), *Cypriana: Old World*, Seattle: Revelore Press, 2017: 163-173.

Tausiet, María, *Urban Magic in Early Modern Spain: Abracadabra Omnipotens*, New York: Palgrave Macmillan, 2014.

Thomás, Pedro Fernades, 'Superstições Populares do Concelho da Figueira', *Boletim da Sociedade Archeologica Santo Rocha* 1 (1904): 25-32.

Vasconcelos, José Leite de, *Etnografia Portuguesa*, vol. 9, Lisbon: Imprensa Nacional-Casa da Moeda, 2007.

Vasconcelos, José Leite de, *Opúsculos*, Vol. 5, Lisbon: Imprensa Nacional de Lisboa, 1938.

Vasconcelos, José Leite de, *Tradições Populares de Portugal*, Porto: Livraria Portuense de Clavel & C.ª – Editores, 1882.

INDEX

B

baptism 46, 48
    of fava beans 44, 45
Barrabás 20, 38, 39, 42, 43
boiling 38, 49
Bolsas de Mandinga 33
Book of St. Cyprian 7-9, 13, 21-23, 39-40, 43, 57
Branco, Camilo Castelo 14, 28
Brazil 20

C

Caifás 20, 38, 39
Carta de Tocar 33
cartomancy 9-14, 16, 22-23, 51-52, 55, 57
Catholicism 21
chamber pot 26-27, 28-29, 30-31, 41
Corpus Christi 37
coscinomancy 38, 41
court cards 10, 11, 42, 51
Creed 13, 31, 35
Crossed Cartomancy 10-11

D

da Ribeira, Catarina 52
da Serra, Antónia 45, 49, 52, 53, 135
de Almeida, Jerónima 47
de Jesus, Maria Rosa 42, 46, 136
de Moura, Paula 35, 37
de Padilha, Maria 20, 39, 42, 43
de Vasconcelos, José Leite 15, 16, 19, 37, 38
Delgado, João 24
Diamonds 47, 64, 66, 74

F

fava beans 49-52. *See also* favomancy
favomancy 43-44, 58
folk oral culture 25. *See also* urban folk magic
forty-card deck 11, 42

G

grimoire tradition 22

H

Hail Mary 31
Hearts 47
hydromancy 22-24, 25, 29, 33, 40-41, 57-58

I

incantations 13-16, 22, 28-29, 45, 50. *See also* seafaring incantation

K

King 42, 47
Knight 47

L

Lisbon 20, 22, 24, 37, 42
Livraria Economica 9
lots. *See* straws
Lots of the Favas 43, 49
Lucifer 38

M

Maria, Domingas 40-42
Marta the wicked 20
materia magica 20

N

novelty 11-13, 22, 42

O

Our Father 31
owl's eyes 39

P

pip cards 10, 11, 51
Portugal 16, 20
Portuguese Inquisition 7, 19, 20, 23, 38, 39, 44

Prayer of St. Cyprian 7, 22
Prosecutor's Notebooks 23
pseudo-hagiography 12, 14, 15, 27, 45

Q

Quimbanda 20

S

Saint Anne 20, 45
Saint Cyprian 7, 20, 22-24, 26-27, 31, 37, 57
Saint Elias 35, 37
Saint Erasmus 20, 28
Saint Friar Isidore 37
Saint Gonçalo 37
Saint Helen 20
Saint John 37, 44, 45
Saint Leonard 20
Saint Mark 35, 37, 38
Saint Odo 39
Saint Simion 24, 115
Satanás 20, 38, 39
seafaring incantation 11, 13-17, 22, 33-34, 40-41
seer 22, 29, 30, 31, 41
Spades 47
Spain 20
straws 22, 26, 27, 31, 41

T

text generation 10, 23, 43, 55, 58-59
Tomás, Pedro Fernandes 13
'the folk' 19

U

Umbanda 20
urban folk magic 20-22, 29, 33, 38-39, 40, 42-43, 46, 57-59

V

virginity 22, 29-30, 41

www.ingramcontent.com/pod-product-compliance
Lightning Source LLC
Chambersburg PA
CBHW031517270326
41930CB00006B/428